HOW TO GROW VEGETABLES INDOORS

2ND EDITION B&W

GINGER BOOTH

ISBN-13: 978-0-9600685-0-0

To Bruce Boatman, fellow online indoor gardening addict, and friend.
Rest in peace, BB.

To Beth, Peat, Jessi,
and all my online gardening friends.

And first, last, and always, to Adrian,
who had to compete with a garden for Mom's attention.

Preface

Preface to the 2nd Edition

It's been 5 years now since *Indoor Salad* was released. Things have changed!

The key change is in lighting technologies. When I wrote the first edition, CFL lightbulbs were everywhere. LED lights were expensive, unreliable, and hard to buy. My experiments growing with LEDs were abysmal failures. But LEDs have come a long way! Now it's CFL lights that are getting harder to buy.

I also expanded the topic of Indoor-Outdoor growing. This includes seed starting as well as bringing crops indoors at the end of the season. I removed the links appendix in favoring of moving that information to my website, where I can maintain it better.

And of course, I keep learning tricks along the way. And in online forums, I continue to learn more about what trips up or confuses the novice.

So this edition has important updates to two topics, and a light dusting of new perspectives throughout. I hope you enjoy!

Preface to the 1st Edition

It's my sister's fault. Back in 2007, she wanted to go in on a present for our mom for Christmas. I'd seen this Really Cool Device on Amazon – an Aerogarden. The sleek little contraption combined grow lights with a hydroponic base, all in a plug-and-play format to cleanly grow herbs and greens on the kitchen counter.

So I bought one for myself, too. I had an Excuse, you see. I justified this $175 tech toy because I'd eat all the lettuce I grew with it. Just think how much thinner I'd be!

I didn't lose much weight.

But I gained one of the most absorbing hobbies ever. Those baby lettuces enchanted me. Growing by my kitchen sink, at chest height, I could watch them develop every step of the way. I took digital pictures for a time-elapsed view. I was hooked.

Before long, I hunted online for a community of fellow devotees. I found an Aerogarden community, but they weren't talking enough. So I haunted the forums, talking to everyone to swell the traffic. I wanted to know what else I could grow in my nifty cool device. Rather than buy 10 of them, I wanted to egg others into trying things, so we could all experiment in parallel. I was delighted when others joined who were going beyond simply using Aerogardens – modifying them, doing other hydroponics, building their own systems. Eventually I left that forum and founded another, aerogardenmastery.com, with some fellow hard-core garden techies.

It's not that I'd never gardened before. Far from it. I can't remember the first time I planted a bean – because I was too small. My gardens weren't much as a kid, because our beach-front yard was too salty and sandy. (Yes, this is a high end problem. Growing up in a beach house was a blast. But plants don't grow well there.) Then I lived in cities, apartments and condos. But in whatever little space I had, I grew flowers every spring.

Then I lived for a half year in Tokyo. In a hotel room the size of a generous walk-in closet. No, I didn't garden there. But I fell in love with Japanese cucumbers. When I got back home, I couldn't buy Japanese cucumbers. Those green waxed torpedo cucumbers in the supermarket, with big seeds and squash guts texture, just weren't good enough any more. So I started container vegetable gardening on my tiny balcony, 30 years ago, because I love cucumbers.

I still grow cucumbers every year. Now I grow them indoors and outdoors. The outdoor cukes last a couple months before succumbing to powdery mildew and cucumber beetles and squash bugs. The indoor cuke vines last up to a year, producing a few cukes a week.

The economic downturn in 2008 caught me freelancing. In the giant game of musical chairs for a good job, I was caught without a seat. With freelance contracts hard to come by, and pay for them plummeting, like so many people, I sought other ways to make a living. Since growing vegetables indoors was a passion, naturally I looked there to develop a product, and even more earnest experimentation began. But I wasn't 100% committed. I'm a web developer, and generally speaking, that's still a safer bet for income than the risk of creating a new business. But I've always wanted to create my own business, beyond the simple work-for-hire freelance life.

Then one evening I went to a networking event – one minute elevator pitches of your business idea. I had four different business concepts mapped out – I tend to over-prepare! I wasn't really sure I'd pitch any of them. But I got up and told them about my system for growing good tomatoes indoors, and how this was a huge demand and product niche not really satisfied by the products already on the market. I won the pitch contest that night, which astonished me.

I was even more surprised by the number of people who said they couldn't help build the business, but they'd sure like to beta test the product. As a consumer product business, this never got off the ground. But the designs for two of those products are included in this book.

With some know-how and ingenuity, you can build your own indoor growing solutions. And deliver them to yourself far more cheaply than I can manufacture and distribute them to you.

Is this information freely available on the web? Most of it. Along with an avalanche of misleading and conflicting information and sales hype. This book also contains solutions I've come up with myself, based on seeing hundreds of my own and other people's experiments. When a fellow entrepreneur in the indoor-crop arena asked me to point him to a single source that explained all this, I couldn't find one.

So this book collects what you need to know to successfully grow crops indoors. With some do-it-yourself projects to get you growing vegetables in your own living room, as cheaply and simply as possible.

I'm in the gardening forums online, by the way. If you see me around, please say hi!

Indoor Salad

Table of Contents

indoor salad

Chapter 1
Introduction

Why grow vegetables indoors?

- Better tasting varieties than the sturdy supermarket standards
- Fresh winter vegetables, not trucked 3,000 miles
- Fresh now – vegetables lose vitamins and flavor within hours of picking
- Could save money, especially if you buy fresh herbs – pricey!
- Indoor grow lights combat seasonal affective disorder (SAD)
- Gardening is deeply satisfying
- Connect with nature as an antidote to urban stress
- Reconnect with your ecosystem because the environment matters to you
- Freshen indoor air and liven up the décor – literally
- Enjoy making things and crafting projects

There are lots of reasons. Or possibly excuses, if you're trying to justify expensive technical and decorating outlays. But probably the most compelling reason to grow food in your home, is because you think "that's cool!"

People who keep pet dogs don't defend their choice. Why should gardeners?

You're not alone. Gardening is one of the most popular pastimes in America and beyond. Go into any big box store – especially in the springtime – and see vast areas dedicated to seeds and gardening gear, pots and potting mix, soil amendments, bulbs and seedling flats. With whole racks of young tomato transplants, that holy grail of the American home gardener – the early, great-tasting home-grown tomato.

But that's in springtime. Outdoors. For people with garden space. Can you have it indoors? Any time of year? Even if you live in a small apartment or condo?

Yes.

Indoor lettuce and kale plants.

But there are a few things you need to know about how to do it. That's what this book is about – how to grow vegetables indoors, as cheaply and easily as possible.

The subject is surprisingly deep. There's a lot to know. But you don't need to know it all to get started. And you don't need to know much about lettuce if what you want is tomatoes. So in organizing this book, each chapter covers first the basics, then gets more detailed. When a chapter gets deeper than your interest at the moment, you can safely skip to the next chapter, and return to basics.

There are also plenty of product vendors out there, who will happily sell you solutions to growing indoor crops. This book includes links to products mentioned. But before you surf the web shopping, I'd like to share one key perspective.

When I began shopping for products to grow vegetables indoors, sticker shock sent me reeling. *Who would buy all this?*

Answer: a marijuana grower. Marijuana has a higher street value than tomatoes.

Do I really need all this? **No**, you don't have to spend $500 or more on an indoor grow tent, complete with fans, humidity controls and meters, 1000 Watt lamp and reflector, convertible between high pressure sodium (HPS) and metal halide (MH) light bulbs, hydroponic system, 5 peculiar bottles of nutrients, etc. You don't even need to know what all that means – though later chapters explain. Yes, the website may show this deluxe system growing *a tomato plant*. Well, tomatoes are legal, aren't they? And the $500 system could grow tomatoes really well.

There are other special considerations for indoor marijuana growing. For instance, in many states, it's illegal. That's changing, but still, indoor plantations are generally hidden in the basement, not on display in a sunny window. Marijuana is a subtropical crop (like tomatoes), with high requirements for light, heat, and humidity for maximal THC concentration – the psychoactive compound in pot bud.

I don't partake or grow this crop myself. I'm curious to know whether my indoor tomato growing tricks work on marijuana – but it's illegal to grow here, and I don't enjoy the stuff.

The point is, those grow systems with the eye-watering price tags are trying to solve a different problem, on a far more lucrative crop.

Avid gardeners do spend amazing amounts of money on tomatoes. One fun book title: *The $64 Tomato: How One Man Nearly Lost His Sanity, Spent a Fortune, and Endured an Existential Crisis in the Quest for the Perfect Garden,* by William Alexander.

Gardeners have to laugh at that title. "Guilty!" But, not that guilty. The Preface covers how I got into all this.

We don't have to go that overboard to grow a great salad indoors at home, year round.

What Can You Grow Indoors?

The short answer is: Anything you can grow outdoors, you can grow indoors.

Of course, some things are harder than others.

Some things, like citrus trees, can be grown "indoors" if you have outdoor sun year round. Crops like wheat and corn could be grown indoors – with 8-plus hours of full sun, provided you also like to keep your house really warm. A watermelon wants that kind of heat, plus 15 square feet of space per fruit. These crops aren't practical for the average home.

The focus in this book is how to grow vegetables in your living room. Or kitchen or bathroom or office – space that people share with the plants. If you have room in a basement or sunny window, or a patch of sun on the balcony, so much the better. But this book is for the urban gardener, sharing their living space with their crops, indoors or out.

So the focus is on crops that are practical, even if sunny windows are in short supply. The most practical indoor vegetables are the same ones you like to eat fresh year round – salad and sandwich ingredients. If you're a gourmet, a steady supply of fresh herbs is also welcome, and saves money over buying them at the market.

The most practical indoor crops are:

- Lettuce and other leafy greens
- Herbs
- Cucumbers
- Peppers – sweet or hot
- Tomatoes

Yes, I've successfully grown all these – and more – indoors. And I've never bought an HID (high intensity discharge) light fixture or a grow tent. Though I've bought more moderately priced home growing appliances.

Can you grow any tomato indoors? No, not unless you have a lot of natural sun available, or invest in serious grow lights. More on that in the tomato chapter. There's an art to choosing the right varieties for indoor growing. Later chapters list tested indoor varieties and other tricks to succeed with these crops, along with similar crops such as eggplant and squash, spinach and green beans.

How Do You Grow Indoors?

Growing indoors, you supply the light, temperature, humidity, water, nutrients, and support that the plants would get outdoors in a well-prepared, well-tended garden bed.

Outdoors, a bounteous Mother Nature supplies all the plant needs. Right?

Well, it might be tempting to get sentimental about how easy all this is to achieve outdoors. But let's not. Outdoor gardens aren't all that easy.

In truth, land prices are exorbitant. Rain and humidity are unreliable. The correct temperatures happen only during specific seasonal windows. Depending on your region, temperatures may be even less reliable than the rainfall. If you grew warm-weather crops only during the 95% certain frost-free months, you might lose 30% of an already too-short growing season. Your cool weather crops can be ruined by heat as well as frost. If you'd like lettuce and tomatoes and cucumbers in your salad, at the same time, you'd soon find that lettuce is a cool weather crop, tomatoes take two or three summer months to start producing, and your hot weather cucumber vines won't survive to the peak of tomato harvest.

Turning the soil, and amending it, can be back-breaking and expensive. Plant supports have to stand up not only to the plants – some vines are tough – but also withstand torrential rains, gale force winds, and whatever other charms your local weather patterns might supply.

And then the true challenge kicks in. The ultimate nemesis in the outdoor garden is usually disease, insects, or other creatures, wild or domestic. Neighbors and local regulations may also curb your outdoor freedom of expression. Or more commonly, all of the above.

Keeping all that in perspective, it's not that hard to grow crops indoors. Most enabling of all, our "practical" crops can thrive in the same temperatures we do, which allows us to grow them indoors year-round.

The other keys to successful indoor growing are loosely divided into the root zone and the leaf zone – what to plant the crops in, and how to get them enough light.

Book Organization

Chapter 2, Plant Tech, introduces our cast of characters – the crops – in a bit more detail. Different crops have different needs, indoors and out. That guides strategy on how best to grow them. But they share common growing techniques. Chapter 3 discusses the root zone options. Chapter 4, Grow Lights, and Chapter 5, DIY Grow Light Projects, cover the challenge of providing enough light indoors.

After covering those basics, Chapters 6 through 8 go into more depth about crop-specific tricks – proven varieties to grow, pruning and harvesting, and specific options in the root and light zones. These chapters can be read in any order.

The book wraps up with indoor/outdoor growing – how to start plants indoors for a longer harvest outdoors. For example, in my area, tomatoes should normally be transplanted outdoors in mid May, to begin harvesting in late July, with ripe red peppers following along in mid August. With indoor growing tricks, I can harvest my first outdoor crops of both in May or June.

Within each chapter, material is arranged from basic to advanced. If it starts getting too deep for your interest, just skip ahead to the next chapter. Come back when and if you want to know more.

Next up, we meet the most brilliant advanced technology in the whole book – the plants themselves.

Chapter 2
Plant Tech

The most marvelous devices we'll discuss in this book are the plants themselves.

Think about it. The magical seed is the tiny dried embryo of a plant, encased in a protective coating. Larger seeds have a food supply packaged on board. The seed can wait on a shelf for up to five years, sometimes even longer, dry and dark. Then water and the right temperature cause it to awaken and grow. As an indoor kitchen gardener, it's a delight to watch this unfold.

Outdoors, at the simplest level, growing this little seedling can be a pretty hands-off affair. With a little guidance, a pre-schooler can grow green beans. Just push the big fat seed into so-so soil with some sun, sometime during the several months of the year when beans will grow in your location. Add water if it doesn't rain enough. The Jack-in-the-Beanstalk story makes a lot of sense, watching the way baby bean plants shoot up.

A pre-schooler can grow bush beans indoors as well, by the way, on a sunny windowsill. (A bush bean is a shin-height variety of green bean. Pole beans easily reach 7 feet [2 m] tall.) She can eat the beans in as little as 6 weeks, too. It's not a hugely productive project – you'd be lucky to get a full serving of beans from a 12" pot. It's fun, though. And little kids love raw green beans, especially if they grew them themselves.

Even with a bush bean and natural sun, though, notice how we've added a little extra tech, here. On the windowsill, you need a pot and potting mix. Adding water is no longer optional. To get a bigger bean harvest, you could also add a soil inoculant – "bean booster" – because the potting mix doesn't contain the microbial symbiotes that help beans fertilize themselves by drawing nitrogen out of the air.

If you don't have the sunny windowsill, you have to replace the sunlight, too.

Water. Nutrients. Substrate (where the roots go). Light.

Outdoors, Mother Nature may supply all of this. In practice, even outdoors, nature can use some help to get good yields. Growing crops indoors, we take nature's place altogether. And alas, most plants aren't as easy to please as the magical bush bean.

Plants have needs. As an indoor gardener, you have to meet those needs. As with people, different strokes for different folks. This chapter is about getting to know these plants a little. Later chapters go into more detail on these plant types. But how to provide for their needs transcends the differences between them.

Greens – the Vegetative Vegetables

That sounds silly, doesn't it? Vegetative vegetables. Technically, "vegetative growth" is the stage between germination (the seed sprouting) and sexual maturity (flowering). In this phase, the little plant is putting all of its energy into growing stem, leaves, and roots. All our crops go through this phase. And most of the vegetative crops will produce flowers and seeds eventually. We just eat them before they get there.

With greens, we eat the vegetative part. We eat the leaves and stems mostly, or sometimes the roots. We don't allow them to mature. We harvest them before they go to seed.

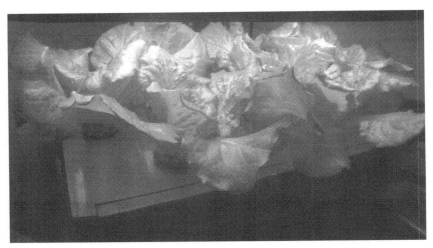

4 week summer crisp lettuce, growing in an Aerogarden.

With greens, the game is grow-grow-grow. These crops are relatively short, and short-lived. Since we eat the leaves, we want to keep them lush and healthy. For most of these plants, light isn't a big issue. Most of them grow well in relatively low light. But the right amount of nutrients, and especially water quality, are critical. The thinner the leaf, the more important humidity is, as well – the water in the air. In bone-dry winter air, a fragile leaf goes limp.For our purposes here, we can separate the vegetative crops into two groups: the ones that can be grown hydroponically, and the ones that can't. It's all about the water with the leafy crops, for better or worse.

Leafy crops can all be grown in soil, of course. So why would you want to grow them hydroponically? Simple – some of them grow much faster hydroponically. The most notable examples are lettuce and basil, which can grow up to twice as fast hydroponically. Hydroponics may also be more convenient than soil, depending on your home circumstances.

Hydroponics and other substrates are covered in Chapter 3, The Root Zone. We'll be more careful about terminology then. For now, let's pretend *"hydroponics"* means *"roots dangle in water."* The point being, some crops thrive on that, but others don't like soggy roots. Let's call the wet-root club *"hydrophilic,"* and the drier-root club *"hydrophobic".*

Hydrophilic crops: Lettuce, leafy brassicas, and leafy herbs.

Brassicas are the cabbage family, including kale, mustard greens, arugula (that's "rocket" for Brits), tatsoi, mizuna, komatsuna, pak choi, and other assorted Asian greens.

Broccoli and cauliflower are also brassicas, and could grow hydroponically. But we eat their flower buds, not their leaves. They don't belong to the vegetative vegetable group.

The *"hydrophilic"* plants are happy to simply dangle their roots in water all the time. This is a mixed blessing. The more happy the plant is in water, the more sensitive it is to high quality water.

Hydrophobic crops: spinach, chard, rosemary, and cilantro.

OK, there's no such thing as a *"hydrophobic"* plant – they all need water. The difference is that these plants don't like their roots wet all the time. They can be grown hydroponically, but not with the simplest "deep water culture" systems. They require a system that periodically provides limited water. Their roots need plenty of air.

Radishes, beets, and carrots are root crops, but grow pretty much the same as leaf crops. For our purposes, they fall into the *"hydrophobic"* camp. Pea shoots are also leafy greens. Rather than grow peas to harvest as peas, you can grow the plants and eat the shoots. Legumes are also best treated as hydrophobic.

To sum up, in vegetative growth, we need mild light, mild nutrients, good water, and the right root environment. For the greens – the *"vegetative vegetables"* – that's all we need. For these plants, continuing on to sexual maturity is called "bolting", and when that happens, the crop quality declines. We eat these crops before they flower. For the plants that go on to sexual maturity – buds and flowers – we need everything to satisfy the vegetative phase, plus different support for the flowering phase.

Cukes and Beans – the Immature Fruits

Cucumbers, summer squash, green beans and peas, are best eaten when still immature and tender. If you've grown them outside, you already know they need almost daily harvesting, to ensure none of the fruit reaches maturity. If an overlooked fruit does mature, the vines shut down and quit producing. Mature fruit flesh is tough, covering large dry seeds.

11 week Korean cucumbers.

And to keep the game fun, the vines are diabolically good at hiding their large fruit. It amazes me that a foot long, two inch diameter cucumber could possibly hide, or a zucchini half the size of a baseball bat. Yet somehow I still miss them sometimes.

This is a high end problem. These crops produce fast. Forget the snail's race to the first ripe tomato, dawdling along four months after planting a seed. With that tomato, after months growing the base plant to first flowering, the fruit takes another 40 days or more to grow from pollinated flower to ripe tomato. A ripe pepper takes longer. In contrast, a good-sized cucumber or green bean can take as little as a week from flower to harvest. Zucchini take mere days. And the pre-flower growing is faster, too. I've harvested first cucumbers in as little as 7 weeks from planting the seed, and bush beans in 6 weeks. Indoors, with space and light at a premium, there's a lot to be said for a crop that produces so fast that you have to check for harvest every couple days.

It's easiest to grow these immature fruits as members of the hydrophobic club. They grow fast and easy in soil. But dangle their roots in water, and the cucumber family suffers root rot. The legume family can host some truly disgusting slimes on waterborne roots. But even if you dodge the slime infestation, beans don't produce much when grown in water. Plastic pots and potting mix are cheap, simple technology. There's little point in spending more and working harder for hydroponics, if the plants grow poorly in water. Though there are hydroponic strategies that work.

Another characteristic of the immature fruit crops is the need to keep growing. Although this is a fruiting crop, you grow it as a vegetative crop. When it finishes the high-growth vegetative phase, its productive life is over. Whatever technique you use to grow them, for best results, never fully switch over to the "fruiting" growth phase regimes you might see discussed online for plants like tomatoes and marijuana.

In practice, the main difference between growing the immature fruit group, over growing the leafy vegetables, is light. By the time they begin flowering, cukes and beans need a lot of light. And picky as they may be about getting their roots too wet when young, eventually cucumbers drink like fish. A cucumber fruit is about 95% water, and the fruit develop fast. Bush beans are compact. Cucumbers and pole beans, however, are very large plants. There are other issues as well, but mostly you get around those by careful selection of what varieties to grow.

Because of their high productivity and short time-to-produce – actually faster than mature lettuce grown in soil – these are some of my favorite indoor crops. I also love to eat them. Cucumber is my favorite vegetable, and raw green beans are my son's favorite. If you have kids at home, try growing green beans with them. Bush beans grow so fast that they're fun to watch, and kids love to eat fresh-picked beans. The only crops faster than bush beans are radishes and certain mini-cabbage type brassicas. Finding a child who's willing to eat those is more of a challenge, though.

As I mentioned in the Preface, I've grown cucumbers for many years outdoors. I've grown them indoors as well, getting up to 100 cucumbers over twelve months, from just two plants. It's nice to have a simple sliced cucumber with dinner a couple times a week. And a cucumber slice does wonders for puffy eyes.

We'll talk more of this high-yield opportunity in Chapter 7, Immature Fruits. There are tricks, of course. But the immature fruits are among the most rewarding crops to grow. And in some ways the easiest.

A word of warning – melons and winter squash are cucurbits, like cucumbers. But they're mature fruits, not immature ones. Melons and winter squash take long

11

months of summer heat. The "winter" part of winter squash – pumpkins, acorn and butternut squash, gourds, etc. – refers to when the crop is harvested (around frost), and how well it stores in a root cellar. But the growing starts at the beginning of summer, then takes until the end of the growing season to mature the harvest. Melons are a bit quicker – they begin and end in the heat of summer. But they need that summer heat. You'll find a lot more cantaloupes from Texas and Guatemala in the supermarket, than from New England and Canada. Melons are harvested mature, so they produce one round of fruit, then end their lives. Winter squash and melons both take a huge amount of garden space, to produce just a few large fruit. Unless you're really determined, melons and winter squash aren't practical candidates for indoor growing.

Tomatoes and Peppers – the Mature Fruits

Did you know that tomatoes and peppers are from the same family as deadly nightshade, or belladonna? Potatoes, eggplant, ground cherries, and tomatillos are also members of the nightshade family – the *Solanaceae*. Tomatoes and potatoes, both New World crops, were initially a tough sell in Europe, because people were afraid they were poisonous. Their leaves are mildly poisonous. We eat the fruits.

For tomatoes, aside from a few fans of fried green tomatoes, we eat the fruit fully ripe. Peppers can be eaten immature or mature, with a major flavor difference between the two. Ripe peppers are also easier to digest, providing far more nutrition and sugars.

The key point about this *"mature"* fruit business is that these crops take a long time.

13 week indoor cherry tomatoes – from seed. Full-size tomatoes take longer.

Pish, you say. You've looked at seed catalogs. They say romaine lettuce takes 70 days. An early girl tomato takes only 60 days.

Yes, well, they're cheating on the count. Days to maturity on lettuce is counted from planting the seed. On the immature fruits, the day count on the seed package seems to count from germination, not planting. With tomatoes and peppers, they count days from transplanting outdoors, which is generally when the plant is already 4 to 8 weeks old. Worse, with the pepper, they're advertising how quickly you can eat it green, not when it's ripe, which takes several weeks longer. And both are quoted under some theoretical optimal conditions. In practice, outdoors or indoors, they're often slower than that, by weeks. Trust me, you could be on your fourth generation of lettuce before you eat your first mid-size tomato. And if you prefer your peppers full-size and ripe, you could sneak in a fifth round of lettuce.

In my experience, eggplant fall somewhere between the immature and mature fruit groups. Eggplant is in the same nightshade family as tomatoes and peppers. But we eat them immature. If you like eggplant, a variety like Fairy Tale is much quicker than peppers or tomatoes, on a conveniently compact plant.

There are no self-pollinating members of the mature fruits group. And you probably don't have any pollinating insects inside your home. So after the same care and feeding you'd give to the other plant groups, you even need to get involved in the sex life of these crops. It's easy enough to do – you just have to shake them gently, or rub the noses sticking out of their flowers. But if you don't, you'll get no fruit.

Summing Up

This chapter was a brief introduction to our cast of characters – the crops covered in this book.

There are other crops in the world. Some of them can even be grown in your living room if you're determined enough. Most can't. Crops that need more than the techniques covered in this book include: corn or other grain; potatoes or other big root crops; artichokes, asparagus, and other perennial crops; melons, winter squash, and other mature cucurbits; fruit and nut trees; and berries.

All of our indoor salad crops start out the same – from a seed. Well, tomatoes and some herbs could be cloned or bought as transplants, but they also start from seed. After that, there are three phases.

Early growth is fast, with relatively low light required. Leafy crops end here – we eat them before they move on to flowering. In the vegetative phase of growth, it's all about the nutrients and water.

Flowering crops require the same as leafy crops, plus much more light. Some varieties may need help with pollination. These are the immature fruits.

Mature fruit crops go through both of those phases, and their nutritional needs change as the crops reach maturity. They always need help with pollination. And in their final ripening phase, they need the most light of all.

The key enabling techniques for growing crops indoors fall into two main areas – the root zone (water, nutrients, and physical support), and light. The next chapter covers the root zone.

Chapter 3
The Root Zone

The first ingredient for growing crops indoors is the *substrate* – what the roots grow in, and how the plant is fed. The childhood method is to plug seeds into the ground and hope for the best.

That level of agricultural technology has been obsolete for nearly 10,000 years. Even outdoors in the ground, you can do better than that. Indoors, you have to do better than that – no rainfall in the living room, for starters.

What do plants need from the root zone?

- Water
- Air
- Nutrients
- Support

Air? Yes, roots need oxygen to grow. We all know that the leaves use carbon dioxide in photosynthesis, and breathe out oxygen. Well, roots don't do photosynthesis – they're not green. Root cells metabolize sugars for the energy they need to live using oxygen, just like we do. If you over-water a plant, so there isn't enough air in the ground, the roots will drown, and even rot. The plant doesn't grow well. Some crops – the ones we dubbed "hydrophobic" in Chapter 2 – grow especially badly, or die.

We have several basic ways to go, to provide these root zone services to indoor crops:

- Pots with standard container potting mix
- Self-watering pots, possibly with advanced substrate materials
- Hydroponic or aeroponic systems

That's really a continuum, not a choice. At one end, we replicate a small bit of ground indoors, and pour water on it from above, to mimic rainfall. At the other end of the spectrum, we've dispensed with the surrogate "ground" altogether. Why? To grow plants better, with higher yields and lower disease, from less effort.

My first real-life introduction to hydroponics – aside from a lifelong addiction to science fiction – was a "Behind the Seeds" tour of the aeroponic gardens at Epcot Center in Orlando. I visited there years before Aerogardens began popularizing home hydroponics. I was enthralled. Bright white clean rooms, with ceilings of glass, bore plants in white piping. The crops were beautiful, and huge. Melons and tomatoes and cucumbers hung down to harvest from overhead trellises. Clean white panels bore lovely heads of lettuce, one per planting hole. The rooms were a balmy 75 degrees or so.

That must have run up a prodigious air conditioning bill, for a greenhouse in the Orlando sun. So that part was certainly Disney showmanship. But the plants and the technology – very real, and absolutely beautiful!

Is that the most cost-effective, convenient way to grow salads in your living room? For some crops yes, for others no. Here again we could spend phenomenal amounts of money for growing systems. But we don't have to. Perfectly viable solutions cost less than $50 – often much less. In practice, most of our salad crops don't greatly care which technology you choose on that continuum, so you simply choose what's cheapest and most convenient for you.

That depends on your circumstances. For instance, I have outdoor in-ground and container crops, as well as indoor crops. I'm no stranger to potting mix. I have a convenient place to dump it, and can wash soil out of pots with a garden hose.

But I've also lived in New York and Dallas and Tokyo, with elevators and third- and fourth-floor walk-ups. Any large growing project involving soil was a nuisance in those conditions. Bags of potting mix are heavy, especially used wet potting mix to be thrown out. I had a half whiskey barrel full of soil for growing cucumbers on my third-floor balcony in Dallas. I inherited it from a third-floor next-door neighbor. You can be sure I left it behind with the apartment – that thing wasn't going anywhere. Washing soil from pots in an urban shower is not convenient, and probably not good for the pipes. A system involving only water is simply easier for urban clean-up.

One place where the choice of root zone strategy isn't just a matter of convenience, is in growing lettuce and herbs. The difference in productivity is just night and day. Growing a romaine lettuce to harvest size in soil takes 75 days, given perfect weather. Growing it hydroponically, you can begin harvesting in 4 weeks. Basil and loose leaf lettuce grow even faster – start harvesting in 3 weeks. Can you grow them in soil? Sure. But if you pay for electric light, or have limited space, soil is less cost-effective for those crops.

There's a lot of hype about all crops growing better hydroponically, and in theory, yes, that should be so. But I've practiced a lot, and with my other salad crops like tomatoes, cucumbers, and peppers, the yield advantages of growing hydroponically aren't very compelling. The plants are designed to grow in soil, after all.

Hydroponic growing can be more cost-effective, at an industrial scale, with well-tended systems carefully fitted to the crop being grown. Most greenhouse crops are grown hydroponically these days. But notice, too, that what's convenient for them is governed by another set of circumstances. In that environment, disease control and waste management are crucial considerations. Just as with my third-floor walk-up, there's a lot of convenience in pouring used nutrients down the drain. Maintaining clean, disease-free, insect-controlled, fertile soil in a large greenhouse is harder.

There's also a style factor to consider. We spend a lot of money on our homes. We want our surroundings at least as attractive and comfortable to us as they are to the plants. In some rooms, you may not care how a crop project looks. But you may be willing to pay more for a beautiful grow-rig, to showcase beautiful plants in a lovely room.

In this chapter we first explore physical substrates – pots and soils – and then introduce hydroponics. At the end, we discuss how organic gardening considerations fit into all this. Later, in the plant-specific chapters, we present some do-it-yourself projects – including the root zone – to get you growing.

The Potted Plant

In the past 10 to 15 years, there's been something of a quiet revolution in gardening – the container garden.

The first gardening book I ever owned was the 1981 first edition of *Square Foot Gardening*, by Mel Bartholomew. Bartholomew had a simple but revolutionary approach. Traditional in-ground row gardening is back-breaking hard work. Rather than prepare a huge garden, not very effectively, he instead built raised beds, prepared the soil thoroughly, and gardened intensively in a tiny area, usually 4x4 foot square. Two decades later, despite this being the best-selling garden book in America, it was still hard to find and buy the ingredients for Bartholomew's special soil mix.

Then container gardening started to take off – in many ways, the square foot method, minus the ground. With only a small spot in the sun, no land ownership required, people increasingly grew vegetables in pots. Ten years ago, it was still difficult to buy some of the ingredients to do these things. For instance, you need a small enough tomato plant to grow in such-and-such a space. But none of the seed sellers told you how big the plant would grow.

But Web 2.0 had arrived, and the customers were talking to each other on the Internet. Enthusiastic gardeners shared pictures, stats, what they'd tried – everything. Now, I get five or six catalogs every year in the mail that sell raised beds, with accessories to extend the season and protect from pests, self-watering containers, and soils specifically mixed for container and raised bed gardening. Now one of my favorite types of large self-watering planter even made it to Home Depot. And because the customers demanded it, if a seed is especially suited for container gardening, that's touted as a feature.

Indoors, in soil, you're essentially doing container gardening under artificial light. The method doesn't need much modification. Here are the basics.

A Self-Watering Pot

In the ground, you pour water over the top of the soil and let it drain down to the roots. But plants grow better if you provide water down below the roots, and let the water wick up through the soil. A pot designed for this is called a self-watering container.

To supercharge this bottom-up watering strategy, in addition to the water at the bottom, fertilizer is added as a side-dressing at the top. With this system, provided the soil wicks water well, you can't over-water the plant, nor over-fertilize it. (Too much fertilizer burns plants.) The plant takes what it needs from the reservoir at the bottom and the fertilizer at the top. Good for the plant, and easy on the gardener. The fertilizer only needs attention once a month or so. This leaves the gardener free to tend the plants themselves.

The bigger the reservoir, the more likely you can leave an adult tomato, pepper, or cucumber for a couple days without a plant-sitter. So go big on the reservoir for big fruiting plants.

You can pick up plastic self-watering pots at Walmart, Home Depot, job lots stores, Amazon – anywhere these days. There are two basic schemes. In one, you pour water into the bottom reservoir through a mouth directly into that reservoir at the bottom of the pot. This opening also lets in plenty of air. If the plant gets too much water from a heavy rain, the water spills out of the same hole.

Most of my pots are this style, for use indoors and out. I like the way they make maximal use of rainwater, which plants love best, while being easy to fill. It's also easy to see how much water is in the reservoir – just stick in a finger. The pots are easy to move around.

Outdoors, I also have three big GrowBox planters, and I'd own more if I had space for them. A GrowBox has the same sort of direct access bottom reservoir, but with a 4 gallon water capacity. It holds a hefty 40 quarts of soil. This planter supports two full-size tomato plants with ease, of the 8 foot tall variety (2.5m). The GrowBoxes would also work indoors. But they're too heavy for me to move. I prefer smaller containers for indoor gardening.

Two full-size tomato plants in a GrowBox outdoors.
Note self-watering reservoir mouth on planter base.

The other main style of self-watering planter has the reservoir sealed inside. You pour water into the bottom reservoir through an access tube at the top. I don't happen to own any of these because I tried the other style first, and I prefer them for my climate. But both styles work. You can even buy kits to insert into a planter or bucket without drainage holes, to turn it into a self-watering container of this type. That might be handy if you had a particular decorating goal in mind, or wanted to construct a self-watering trough to fit into a specific area. The well-known EarthBox is the top-filled version of the GrowBox size planter. I've seen an even bigger patio planter of this type at Home Depot, possibly twice the size of a GrowBox.

Plastic pots actually work better than clay pots. But if it's important to your décor, clay pots can also work. If there are enough drainage holes, you could place the pot in a deep saucer, and pour water into the saucer. That's too small a reservoir to use only bottom-watering, however – you'd likely have to water from above as well.

Another approach is a grow bag, as opposed to a plastic pot. I haven't experimented with that indoors, but it could work. It's important, though, that the reservoir fit the planter rather closely, without too much light falling on the water. Well-lit, fertile water grows algae. Plants do not like algae water.

If you don't use a self-watering pot, and plan to pour all the water in from the top, it's doubly important that the pot have good drainage.

A Pot of the Right Shape and Size

Probably the most common mistake in container gardening – one I've certainly made – is to grow a plant in an inappropriate size or shape of pot. We cover the depth and volume of soil needed for assorted plant types in the later plant-specific chapters.

Preview: The rule of thumb for tomatoes is a 5 gallon pot, 20 liters of soil.

Many books and websites on container gardening likely also cover this. And *Square Foot Gardening* gives a rough idea of the maximum close packing of plants. Most plants can be grown closer together than described on a seed packet, if you're taking care of them intensively.

Container Potting Mix

We already touched on this. For a self-watering pot, you need a fairly porous, light, fluffy potting *mix*, not *soil.* Soils are too heavy. Non-obviously, stay away from anything called *moisture control* – those mixes tend to get soggy and stay soggy. The organic choice styled products I've tried were also poor at wicking water. But if you'd prefer the organic-soil feature, you could buy perlite to mix into the organic potting mix to lighten it.

Perlite is a puffed volcanic glass – like rice krispies – which qualifies as organic. We talk a bit more about *"organic"* toward the end of the chapter. There are potting mixes made especially for container gardening, and these might be a good choice. I've honestly never found anything that worked better than ordinary Miracle Gro potting mix, and most other options are more expensive.

Be aware of how much fertilizer is already in the potting mix. Seedlings don't want extra fertilizer. When the plants are bigger, you can add some fertilizer, sparingly. We talk more about plant-specific requirements in later chapters.

You can also use soil-free mixes, or cut any potting mix with inert materials like perlite, vermiculite, or coco coir, the fiber from coconut husks – a highly renewable resource. The less nutrients there are in the potting mix, the more you need to add them some other way, either with fertilizer or with hydroponic nutrients in the water. For my big potato growing bags (outdoors), I mix leaf compost from the town recycling center with potting mix and perlite, to save the money and waste of filling them with such huge quantities of potting mix – each grow bag takes about 10 gallons. I don't use leaf compost indoors because I'm leery of bringing in insects.

Plain old potting *mix* from the big box stores works fine. Garden *soil* does not.

Fertilizer

There are lots of fertilizer approaches. All work well, so long as you don't over-fertilize, which burns the plants. The simplest is probably a shake-and-feed style product – little kernels of fertilizer intended to be strewn across a garden, and worked into the soil slightly, that release nutrients over months. I've successfully used Osmocote, Miracle Gro Shake-n-Feed, and Dynamite Plant Food. The latter brand is especially eco-conscious and has organic formulations, tomato formulations, etc. When the plants are big enough to need extra fertilizer, just make one or more depressions in the potting mix at the top of the pot, and add the proper sized spoonful of fertilizer granules. Press it in a bit, so the plant roots can reach it, and water in. That way the plant can take what it wants, without getting more than it can handle.

The excellent GrowBox and EarthBox fertilizers can also be bought independently of those containers, and placed in a clump at the top of your own pot the same way, with the quantity scaled to the amount of crops in the pot. Be careful of doing this with big plants like tomatoes, though. Plants grow huge on these fertilizers. Even outdoors, providing enough light and support for an 8-foot tomato vine (2.5m) is a challenge.

Alternatively, if you have hydroponic nutrients, you could add those to your potted projects – mixing a rather weaker solution than you would for straight hydroponics. The less soil in your potting mix, the more it makes sense to use hydroponic nutrients. All fertilizers provide the bulk nutrients plants use – nitrogen, phosphorus, and potassium (N-P-K). Fewer provide the micro-nutrients plants need – magnesium, boron, copper, iron, manganese, molybdenum, and calcium. Hydroponic nutrients are designed to supply everything but the water.

Mulch

"Mulch" is simply something that covers the soil at the top of your pot. Indoors, mulch is optional. There are a couple reasons you might want to use it, though – insect suppression, and algae suppression.

The most common insect pest of indoor potted plants is the fungus gnat – little black flying bugs. They do some harm to the plants, with larvae nibbling at the roots. But mostly, it's annoying to have black bugs flying around your home. This insect alone is enough to make some prefer hydroponics to container growing for indoor vegetables. Mulching the top of your pot can help suppress the population, though it won't solve an outbreak.

If the top of the soil is wet, fertilized, and getting lots of light, it will grow algae. Algae is not good for the plants. You can let the top of the soil dry out between watering. This is good for the plants, and also helps curb insects. But mulching keeps light off the soil, so algae can't grow.

For mulching, you can use newspaper, outdoor mulch (preferably insect-free), hydroton grow rocks, perlite, vermiculite, trash bag plastic, supermarket brown bag, pretty pebbles, or nearly anything that keeps light off the soil. If desired, you add mulch after your seedlings are emerged and thinned, keeping the mulch spaced a bit away from the stems.

One caveat: hydroton grow rocks – expanded clay pellets – are very popular for indoor hydroponic gardening. But they can suck the moisture out of thin lettuce leaves, when used as mulch. If you're growing a low-slung plant, try to use a non-absorbent mulch.

Water

We're all blessed with whatever local water supply we have. Use the best water you've got for best results. Like many in the U.S., my tap water is *hard,* meaning it has a lot of dissolved calcium carbonate – limestone. It's also dosed with chlorine – that's bleach – to kill microbes, especially in summer.

If you leave a gallon of water out for a few hours or a day, most of the chlorine will out-gas from the water, which helps. Using a drinking water filter makes water taste better, but can't remove the calcium hardness. If you have an aquarium for fish, you probably already have a pretty good idea whether your water is suited for growing. If it's not good for fish, it won't make your plants happy either.

We'll talk more about water in the hydroponics sections, where its quality is even more important. For now, suffice it to say that your available water quality may limit your growing results. To start, just use tap water. Once the plants are growing, if you suspect you have a problem, buy a gallon of distilled water (not "spring" water), and see if the plants react favorably. If they do, maybe your water supply could use improvement.

Transplanting

Growing indoors, your brightly lit area will always be in limited supply. And artificial lights consume a lot of power. To grow the most vegetables I can indoors, I usually start my plants in more compact pots, or some other scheme, while a previous crop completes its useful life cycle in the big pots under the bright lights. Some plants are more transplant-tolerant than others – we get into that in the plant-specific chapters later. For now, just note that you don't have to use a giant pot for a baby plant.

Of course, some baby plants turn into large plants faster than others.

Summing Up Potted Plants

We covered a lot of ground here, so let's circle back and summarize the basic scheme.

Buy a self-watering planter of the right size for your growing project. Fill it with a light potting mix – ordinary Miracle Gro potting mix (no moisture control or organic) works as-is, and is available almost everywhere in the U.S. year-round. Follow instructions on the pot for watering the soil the first time. Generally you fill it in stages, watering in each layer as you go, to get the water wicking upward properly. Insert a transplant or seeds, and water again. Fill the reservoir. For hydrophobic crops, refill the reservoir when the reservoir runs dry. For water-loving crops, you can keep the reservoir topped up, but letting it run dry helps control insects. Make sure the plant gets enough light.

Everything else is finesse.

Finesse tends to be crop-specific. For instance, tomatoes prefer less acid and cucumbers prefer more. So more about finesse in the plant chapters.

For most crops, growing a potted plant is so easy, cheap, and yields such good results, that I don't bother with anything more complicated any more. Been there, tried that, pots are simpler. But there are other crops (and other circumstances) where hydroponics really work better.

On to the hydroponic root zone.

Hydroponics

Hydroponics! Ooh, scary word, right? It doesn't have to be. Let me show you my simplest hydroponic system:

Park Starts seed starter block with 7 tomato seedlings (rear)
and calibrachoa cuttings (front – it's a flower).

That is a small chunk of styrofoam, with spongy plugs in most of its 18 holes. It sits in a tray of water enriched with some seedling fertilizer. In this picture, the compact block held seven baby tomato plants in back, and nine calibrachoa cuttings in front. (Calibrachoa is a flower, sort of a trailing mini-petunia, usually grown from clones, not seeds.) This system, called "Park Starts Seed Starters", comes with three styrofoam blocks, complete with seedling fertilizer and 54 sponges, for $12 at Park Seed. Plus shipping.

And yes, *that* is a hydroponic system. Granted, it's a very small one, and all of those plants soon graduated to something bigger.

What makes a system hydroponic is that the roots grow in some substrate other than soil, and are fed a nutrient solution – in this case, seedling fertilizer mixed in water. The substrate itself is inert – the sponges. The sponges provide physical anchoring for the roots, and a good balance between holding air and water. All the plant nutrient responsibility is removed from the fertile soil, and transferred to the water solution.

Why do that? Well, it's a lot easier to control what and how much the plants are fed. You can tailor the nutrients to suit the plant, and to the specific life stage of the plant. Seedlings – and lettuce – take little fertilizer. The vegetative growth phase, focused on growing leaves and roots, needs generous levels of nitrogen. The fruiting phase takes less nitrogen, but more magnesium and sulfur. At any phase of life, too much fertilizer harms the plants. It's called *fertilizer burn*. The plants need frequent fresh water anyway. It's easier in some ways to mix the fertilizer – nutrients – into the water, instead of trying to work it into the soil without damaging the roots.

Some plants – not all – can also take advantage of the easy-feed nutrient solution. They put less energy into growing root mass, and more into growing leaves and fruits. As with the humble little seedling block in the photo, most seedlings germinate and grow faster hydroponically. And they grow more safely. Soil contains many microbes, some of which can kill a seedling. With few roots yet, a seedling can't withstand its soil drying out even for a few hours. Yet if it gets too much water, the roots drown. The particular tomato plants in that picture went into small pots of potting mix after two weeks. But for their first two weeks, they were safer in the seedling block. They took up little space, germinated quickly, grew a nice set of starter roots and leaves, and got off to a good start.

The air part isn't obvious, but roots need air as well as water, to support their metabolism. We all know that plants breathe in carbon dioxide and breathe out oxygen. That's actually the leaves, though, carrying out photosynthesis. Roots live in the dark, do no photosynthesis, and need oxygen the same as we do. Their energy comes from metabolizing the sugars created by the leaves in photosynthesis. That takes oxygen.

For the simple seed starting block, providing air isn't difficult. When the roots grow out the bottom of the block, you sit the block ajar except when watering. Air can soak through the root sponge, top and bottom. Without air, roots drown and die. If the roots dangle in water, the nutrient solution has to provide not just water plus nutrients, but also aeration.

The main difference between hydroponic systems is how air gets to the roots. No air equals stunted plant growth.

You may recall from Chapter 2 that one of the important things to know about the crops you're growing, is how wet-tolerant their roots are. Part of that is a greater need for air on the part of the *"hydrophobic"* crops. But there are other reasons. For instance, cucumber roots tend to rot in water. They can live and grow with inadequate half-rotted root mass – until they try to ripen some fruit. The sudden huge water demand of developing a fruit, causes the plant to collapse and die. This doesn't mean you can't grow cucumbers hydroponically – you can. But they don't grow well in the type of hydroponic system where the roots simply hang in a tub of aerated nutrient solution.

The technical name for such a tub system is *deep water culture* (DWC), or *passive hydroponics.* This isn't the only type of hydroponics. But it is the easiest to make for yourself and the cheapest to buy. The water is aerated the same way aquarium water is aerated. An air pump feeds into an airstone – a bubbler – in the nutrient reservoir. Non-obviously, it's the bubbles popping at the water surface that oxygenates the water.

More advanced hydroponic systems include ebb and flow systems, drip systems, aeroponics, and aquavalve-based systems.

Ebb and flow systems place the roots in a spongy medium sitting in a tray. Blocks of rock wool are popular sponges for this. At intervals, a nutrient solution is pumped into the tray. The sponges soak up some, then after a little while the excess solution is drained out of the tray. Automated pumps repeat the cycle several times a day. Ebb and flow systems are also called ebb and flood, or flood and drain.

Commercial systems may recycle the drained nutrient solution, pumping it back into the reservoir for the next flow phase. Large installations may insert an ultraviolet light microbe-killing step to this recycling. Or, they "drain to waste" – the nutrient solution goes through the system once, and drains into the sewer. The latter may seem wasteful, but if the cycle pumps back to the reservoir, there is additional effort to keep the correct nutrient concentration and cleanliness in the reservoirs. Most hydroponic greenhouse agriculture uses ebb and flow systems. In January, if you're eating a truly ripe tomato, or a cucumber from Canada, it was probably grown with ebb and flow hydroponics in a greenhouse. Small ebb and flow systems start around $90.

The price ranges I'm quoting here are just for hydroponic hardware. The consumable materials – substrate, nutrients, and power, if needed – would be in addition, as are lights, if needed.

In a drip system, the plant nestles in a sponge, and the sponge nestles into some other substrate in a plastic basket. Typical substrates are hydroton grow rocks – clay pellets – or coco coir, the fiber from coconut husks. Nutrient solution is dripped from the top, wets the roots and substrate, and drains into a reservoir at the bottom. A pump cycles the reservoir back up to drip at the top.

Windowfarms drip-based hydroponic system, 6 hanging units.
Not for sale at this writing, but you can DIY.
(Photo used with permission, Windowfarms).

In an aeroponic system, the nutrient solution is misted onto the roots, which hang in the air. Most of the gorgeous plants I saw at the Epcot Center exhibition were aeroponic. A downside to aeroponics is that nutrients tend to crystallize out of solution and clog up the misting nozzles. But with an excellent air / water / nutrient mix, and other advantages such as reduced plant-to-plant disease transmission and lower water use, aeroponics may be the best of all hydroponic systems. The least expensive aeroponic systems I've seen cost around $200. A friend online built one slightly less expensively, starting from buying the misting nozzles and pumps. But that's quite a project, and he already owned the tools.

The aquavalve (Autopot) is a device that passively controls mini-flooding, by opening a valve as a substrate mat dries out. With the valve open, nutrients flow down a tube from a reservoir, and wet the substrate, and the valve shuts off again. So it has the the flood, but not the drain, of a flood and drain system. This is a gravity-fed system, requiring no electricity – water flows downhill when the valve is open. I haven't tried one of these systems yet, but I've had friends online who used it successfully, and I want one. Aqua-Pots (Easy2Gro system) run about $40 and up. Or you can buy the valves for about $25 and devise your own system around them.

Probably the easiest entry-level novice hydroponic system you can buy is an Aerogarden, from AeroGrow. Aerogardens combine deep water culture with on-board grow lights, all in a compact unit. No, Aerogardens are not aeroponic – they're deep water culture. These all-in-one systems cost from $50 - $600, depending on the size of unit and current deals. I love these systems and have owned six of them. Their compact fixed sizes are rather limiting, but there are ways around that. The Aerogarden's formula for success is to guarantee your success. The all-on-one aspect includes it all – nutrients, seed kit, sponges, lights, automated operation. If the crop fails, AeroGrow will offer growing advice, and send you a new kit. A lot of people, myself included, started growing indoor crops with an Aerogarden. The more adventurous, including myself, went on from there. It's a great place to start, though not the cheapest.

There are other deep water culture (DWC) systems that provide the base reservoir and aeration pump, without the lighting solution. These can be cheaper, and generally provide a bigger reservoir (tub of nutrients). The fact that they don't include on-board lights, is actually an advantage if you want to grow bigger crops like full-size peppers and tomatoes. By detaching the lights, you can give the plants more room. Prices run from about $45 on up. Some of the Stealth Hydroponics systems on Amazon look like a sound buy, though I haven't tried them personally.

You can also build your own. I considered describing how for a do-it-yourself chapter. But the truth is, if you can buy one already made for less than $50, and more beautiful ones for $100, it makes little sense to make your own. Better to buy the first one, learn how it works while using it, and then devise your own based on the experience.

Stealth Hydroponics systems, growing collard greens, kale, and Swiss chard.
Photo courtesy of R.W. Pochciol, Pennsylvania.

Hydroponic Gotchas

There are a couple issues to keep in mind, common to all hydroponic growing. The system might leak. And you can't allow light into the water.

The first is obvious when you think about it. Any system with a multi-gallon tub of water, especially with a drain hole near the bottom, could leak. If the tub holds five gallons, you have a five gallon puddle waiting to happen.

You can add sealant, or caulking. You can tape all around the junctures. But sooner or later, it may leak. In practice, this is just as true growing in soil, because you'll spill water. If your grow system uses electricity, it's crucial that water doesn't run into the power outlet.

A power cord, to a water-reservoir system, needs to dip below the level of the power outlet, then come back up to the plug. Spilled water will follow a power cord to its lowest point, then drip down from there. That lowest point must not be the power outlet. Since you and the water both conduct electricity, be careful around the power plug when cleaning up a spill.

Even if a hydroponic system doesn't use power, indoors you have furnishings to protect. The more gallons are involved, the greater the potential damage to carpets, drywall, woodwork, etc. So your growing area needs some thought as to waterproofing. And when comparing the option of building your own system, vs. buying one ready-made, note that making the system watertight is a crafting challenge.

The need to keep the water dark may not be so obvious. Any tub of water, especially nutrient-enriched, will grow algae if exposed to light. Algae is green slime. You want to grow vegetables, not green slime. Algae steals the air from the nutrient solution. Algae also releases chemicals that your crop plants object to. Essentially, algae poisons your nutrient solution, and your plants. Your grow lights, or sunny window, are working hard to provide light to your plants. Your hydroponic system needs to keep that light out of the water. Or you'll grow green slime, instead of healthy plants.

√ **Tip:** Hydrogen peroxide kills microbes, and oxygenates water.

If you suspect microbes are getting out of hand in a nutrient reservoir, add a tiny amount of hydrogen peroxide, maybe a teaspoon per gallon. At very low concentrations, peroxide increases the oxygenation of the nutrient solution and kills algae and other microbes, without harming the plant roots.

Hydroponic Nutrient Solution – the Water

In hydroponic growing, it's all about the water. That may seem obvious. But 100% pure pristine water is hard to come by. Your tap water already has stuff in it, before you add hydroponic nutrients. My tap water has so much stuff dissolved in it, that I collect rainwater for my hydroponic crops. My plants are emphatic that rain water is better.

This is a nuisance, to put it mildly. Tap water is far more convenient. On some crops, like tomatoes or cucumbers, I can get away with using my tap water most of the time, with other compensating tricks, if rainfall has been lacking. Other crops, like lettuce and brassicas (the cabbage family, including kale, mustard, pak choi, etc.) hate my tap water, and visibly fail to thrive on it.

In fact, after noticing how thoroughly my first indoor brassicas hated our water, we noticed that we people didn't much care for our new condo's tap water, either. I bought a water filter. After three days of drinking our water filtered, our taste buds revived from the dead. We could taste our food again. Occasionally I run this experiment backwards – I forget to change the water filter. It's not my imagination. Food tastes better within days, each time I replace an overdue water filter.

We tested the water then, of course. What on earth was wrong with my pipes? But nothing was wrong. It's just very *hard water.* With plenty of chlorine and fluoride added, too, depending on the season. The regional water authority adds chlorine to manage the microbial load in the water supply. It smells like – and essentially is – chlorine bleach. The fluoride is a public health measure to encourage healthy teeth. My cheap Brita water filter does a good job of getting rid of the bleach, and making the water taste better. But no water filter can correct hard water.

Hard water has a high level of calcium carbonate dissolved in it. This mostly comes from dissolved limestone in ground water. Many regions have hard water – it's just a fact of life of your local water supply. You can't remove calcium carbonate by filtering, just as you can't filter the salt from sea water.

Why is this is a problem? Plant roots take up nutrients by *osmosis* – dissolved nutrients cross into the plant across cell membranes. Calcium is a nutrient that plants metabolize, just as salt is a nutrient that humans use. What happens when a person drinks salt water when they're thirsty? They get the water they need. But unfortunately, they get too much salt along with it. The person's only way to get rid of the excess salt is to flush it out with water. Drinking more salt water just makes you dehydrated and thirstier. This is a rough analogy, but it works to understand the plant's basic problem when growing in hard water. Even if the water is hard, yes, the plant can still take up nutrients. But for each sip of what it needs, it gets too much of what it doesn't want and can't get rid of. So it doesn't grow as well.

Another aspect of the plants taking up nutrients by osmosis, is that for each type of plant, there's a limit to the total dissolved concentration of all ingredients that it can handle. There are assorted ways to measure dissolved concentration. I normally measure *electrical conductivity,* or EC, and have a deluxe EC meter given to me as a gift. Lettuce, for example, grows best with an EC of around 1.6. The EC of my tap water, before adding any nutrients at all, is about 0.3. So if I make up a batch of nutrients to an EC of 1.6, nearly 20% of the stuff dissolved in the water is stuff the plants don't want. They're not well-fed, yet they can't handle nutrients any stronger.

My nifty EC measuring device, by the way, was a BlueLab Truncheon. This measures only EC – you'd need another device to measure pH, which is the acidity or alkalinity of the water. The truncheon costs about $100, and it sure is nice. I received mine as a hugely generous gift, from an online indoor gardening friend, for I never would have justified buying one for myself. To measure EC, you simply dip a wand into the water. Is it a must-have? No. There are cheaper nutrient meters available to explore, and unless there's a problem, you can manage without any meter. But BlueLab is the best, and I was very sad when mine died.

Hard water also tends to have too high a pH for plant growth. Most plants take up nutrients best with slightly acidic water. With neutral pH (neither acidic nor basic) being 7.0, most plants prefer a mildly acidic pH of around 6.0. Some like it a little more acid – cucumbers seem to enjoy acid fertilizer now and then. Careful here – pH is a logarithmic scale, not a linear one. "A little more acid" than 6.0 might be 5.8, while 5.0 is an order of magnitude more acidic than 6.0. Tomatoes prefer their water a little sweeter, around 6.5, and some crops – such as spinach and chard – even prefer slightly basic soil, with a pH above 7.0. Lime, calcium carbonate, is used to make soil more basic – the same stuff that makes water hard.

My hard tap water ranges up to a pH of 8.2, which is too alkaline for indoor salad crops. I'm not aware of any crops that prefer a pH as high as 8.2. Grass might like it. Fortunately, the hydroponic nutrients themselves lower pH. They assume water starts at a neutral pH of 7.0, and at normal formulations, the nutrients would bring that down to around 6.0 pH, which is ideal for most plants. If the starting water is not at a neutral pH, you can buy a pH kit to adjust it by adding base or acid until the nutrient solution reaches the 6.0 to 6.5 pH range. It takes some fiddling.

Rain water is generally close to a perfectly neutral pH of 7.0.

There are ways to remove calcium carbonate – hardness – from water. But they are neither easy nor cheap. And they tend to be wasteful, either in energy or wasted water.

One way is to distill the water. When you convert water to water vapor – boil it – the calcium carbonate is left behind. The water vapor is condensed back into water in a separate container, without calcium carbonate in it. You can buy a nifty device that distills water for you, or buy distilled water by the gallon. Aquarium owners do it all the time. It takes energy to boil water.

Another way to remove hardness is reverse osmosis. I won't go into the details. The Internet can provide an explanation if you're interested. I've never owned an RO system myself. But they generally produce 1 gallon of fairly pure water for every 5 to 20 gallons they discard to waste. They can be installed to purify all the water coming out of your kitchen tap, or even on the water main for your home, if desired.

And then there's rain water, which is naturally distilled, plus whatever it picks up from air pollution, birds on the roof, rain gutters, and flying storm debris. I put a dish tub under the gutter spout. It holds 2.5 gallons of water. I decant it into 1 gallon water jugs and 2 liter soda bottles. To keep algae and mosquitoes from growing in it, I harvest the rainwater fairly promptly. Rather manual and low-tech, but it's free, clean enough, and the plants love it. Someday I'd like a rain barrel to automate this and hold enough water for the outdoor gardens in the non-freezing months. In the winter, I'd still have to use the gutter-and-dish-tub method, though. A rain barrel would burst if allowed to freeze.

Hydroponic Nutrients

Many nutrient products are available on the market, and they all come with instructions. This section is a basic introduction.

Nutrients – nutes – are sold with several different packaging strategies: one-part, two-part, and three-part. The one-part nutes may come in liquid or dry form. In addition to the base nutrients to support plant growth, vendors offer a bewildering array of additives, to promote this or that. Probably the most important thing to know about all those, is that they're *additives*, not the base nutrients that support plant growth.

In keeping with their all-in-one product line, Aerogarden offers one-part nutrients. Regardless of what you're growing, and what phase of plant growth, you use the same nutrients, maybe with a different dosage amount, catered to the size of the Aerogarden nute reservoir. Their instructions are to simply add more water when the reservoir level gets low, and add more of the 1-part nutrient once every two weeks. Though they advise a "rinse and refill" of the reservoir with fresh water once a month when growing more demanding plants, like tomatoes. This works, and is undeniably simple.

You can get better crop growth by working a bit harder, even with one-part nutrients. Doing a rinse and refill every week, for any crop, yields more luxuriant growth. This is especially important when the plants are able to drink the reservoir dry in less than a week. This costs more in nutrients and effort, but gives higher yields from healthier plants.

Depending on what's growing, it may be easy to simply pour out old nutrients into the sink, add a little fresh water and swish, dump again, and refill with nutes. With large plants that need support, this isn't convenient, and might damage the plants. There are hand pumps on the market for emptying out liquid in situ. But I find a simple siphon works better. Place a drainage container on the floor below the reservoir to be drained. Gravity does the work, so the source reservoir has to be above the drainage container.

You don't have to suck on the siphon. Completely fill a length of air hose with water, and seal it with a finger on one end, to keep the water from pouring out. You can buy air hose at any aquarium supply store, including some Walmart stores. Secure the other end of the siphon down into the drainage container, then submerge the sealed end into the bottom of the higher reservoir, and let go your sealing finger. The liquid drains downward through the siphon hose.

I don't usually bother with rinsing, just draining. But if the nutes smell funny, after draining, you could add some clear water, swish gently so as not to disturb the roots too much, and drain again. Then refill with fresh nutes.

Back to our tour of nutrient options. One of the oldest – and still best – nutrient products is the three-part Flora series from General Hydroponics. This comes in three bottles of concentrate – FloraMicro, FloraGro, and FloraBloom. With this system, and those like it, you mix up nutrients by adding the concentrates to water, in different proportions based on the life stage of the plants to be grown.

Wouldn't it be more convenient to just mix the nutrients together, and then measure the mix into the water?

No. The nutrients need to be added to water in the correct order. Otherwise they react with each other in something called *nutrient lockout*. The net result is that the nutrients in the water aren't usable by the plants. So when making these multi-part nutes, add the concentrates to the water in the correct order. And never mix the concentrates together directly – only as diluted. Add FloraMicro to the water first, then add the FloraGro and FloraBloom in either order. The details may vary between particular three-part and two-part products, but the gist remains the same – mix them in order, diluted in the water. Don't mix the concentrates together directly.

To measure, I use an ordinary dosing syringe, left over from an oral antibiotic prescription once upon a time. You can buy a dosing syringe at the pharmacy, or the pharmacist might be willing to give you a freebie. When mixing nutes, be sure to rinse the syringe in between concentrates. For example, measure the FloraMicro, squirt into the water, rinse, then measure FloraGro, so as not to contaminate the FloraGro concentrate with the residual FloraMicro on the syringe.

I've been happy with the GH Flora system, and when it comes to this general type of product – multi-part liquid concentrate nutrients – I've just stuck with them. It's a flexible system that meets my needs. It's widely popular, and most of the online forums have other users of the system. So it's easy to understand what other people are doing, and repeat their experiments. So I haven't experimented as much with the competing multipart systems. But there are other perfectly good nutrient makers out there, with three-part and two-part concentrates. Some feature organic formulations, with sea kelp or fish – there's lots of variety. Lots of people prefer organic nutrients. More on that in the next section.

I tried a dry one-part nutrient formulation for tomatoes once, thinking that would be more convenient than the liquid three-parter. The product I tried really didn't work as well, and wasn't any more convenient. Measuring one nutrient was simpler. But the resulting pH was too low (the solution was too acidic). So then I had to do a second more tedious step of pH correction, or my plants' leaves got lesions, and probably suffered acidic root damage. These days, being lazy, I use a one-part organic nutrient for tomatoes. Less hassle, works great.

I currently use another one-part vegetative dry nutrient for lettuce, MaxiGro, mixed at a weak concentration. It's cheap and easy and grows well. The same company that makes my organic tomato nutes, Urban Farm Fertilizers, also offers a vegetative growth liquid nutrient.

What won't work well is growing crops hydroponically in a *fertilizer* solution – like, MiracleGro in water. Fertilizer is not the same thing as *hydroponic* nutrients. Fertilizer is made to enrich soil, primarily with N-P-K – nitrogen, phosphorus, and potassium. Flowers and food crops deplete these macro nutrients from soil, and fertilizers are meant to add them back. But most fertilizers don't provide the other trace minerals needed to support plant growth – calcium, copper, zinc, boron, iron, manganese, etc. If you grew seeds in a weak MiracleGro solution, it would appear to work at first. But the plants would not thrive as they would if grown in hydroponic nutrients formulated to be a plant's sole mineral source.

Note that here I'm speaking of the popular dry green MiracleGro add-to-water fertilizer product, not MiracleGro potting mix. The potting mix works fine indoors – I use it all the time.

As for all the other nutrient additives – experiment if you want. The additives are not the basic building block hydroponic nutrients that you need as a base to feed your plants. I haven't played with the bonus additives, but you might find they do wonderful things.

Are these nutrients safe, to have in your home? Yes. They aren't good to drink, of course. Make sure your cat doesn't use a nutrient reservoir as a water bowl. But they're probably safer to have around the house than most cleaning supplies. When in doubt, read the label for warnings.

One more introductory point on hydroponic nutrients. Many feel that hydroponically grown produce tastes vapid, flavorless compared to the soil-borne plants. And it's true that it's easier to get good flavor from soil-grown plants. But you can improve the flavor of some hydroponic fruits by increasing the concentration of nutrients a little when the fruits are ripening. This is the hydroponic equivalent to watering less. Many fruits – tomatoes, peppers, and melons, for instance – taste better if you water less as they reach harvest. This is finesse, a trick to improve your crop, once you've got the basics down. You can grow great-tasting peppers and tomatoes indoors, hydroponically or in a pot.

Growing Organically

Is "organic" produce important to you? Food without mysterious chemicals and murderous herbicides, pesticides, and fungicides?

You're not alone. An ever-increasing motivation for home-grown produce – indoors or out – is to get real food, minus the artificial and possibly dangerous chemicals. Real food tastes good and is good for you. Strange chemicals, not so much. Strange chemicals used as herbicides and pesticides are particularly worrisome, even if you're not a close relative of the dandelion or cucumber beetle.

Hydroponic growing may seem at odds with that goal at first. Aren't we using mysterious and possibly dangerous chemicals? Well, no. The mysterious, worrisome type of chemicals tend to have long unpronounceable names and complex molecular structures. N, P, and K are not mysterious chemicals – they are chemical elements. Nitrogen is the largest component of the air we breathe. None of the ingredients in standard hydroponic nutrients are complex, scary compounds. Most of them are elemental. Are they organic? No. In fact, all the nutrients plants use – N, P, K, trace elements, sunlight, water – are inorganic. The plants turn these inorganic building blocks into organic compounds. They create themselves, life, out of inorganic materials.

So when we describe organic growing, we're not using the term in a chemical sense, but in more of a provenance sense. Organic hydroponic nutrients are in some sense produced in a more natural way, via biological rather than chemical processes. Usually this involves seaweed extracts, guano, and fish. Organic nutrients likely have more impurities, not less, than their more chemically precise nutrient competitors.

Half of my experience is with the more chemically purist nutrients for hydroponics – the General Hydroponics Flora series in particular. I started there, and it's the gold standard. But lately I've also been using organic nutrients, interchangeably. If you feel strongly about it, experiment. Poke around online and grant your business to environmentally responsible companies, nutrients produced from good stuff, etc. One suggestion, though – when shopping, look for online reviews that mention how the organic formulation smells. And how easy it is to clean off your equipment. Clean and clean-smelling are important to me, in my kitchen, office, and living room. I grew up on the shore. I love the scent of fish and seaweed, in its place. That place is not a science experiment in my kitchen.

But aside from that squeamish little reservation, using organic nutrient formulations ought to work great. I'm not persuaded that the nutrients are more available to plant growth in the hydroponic case. But if the nutes get good reviews, the nutrients are available enough for the product to work. It grows healthy plants.

In potting mix, the organic argument is a little different. A truly organic, rich soil outdoors is alive with fungi, worms, beneficial bacteria, insects – a complete living and breathing ecosystem. This ecosystem provides services to the plant roots, symbiotic relationships, disease moderation. Nutrients in this living soil are easily available to roots, to support riotous plant growth.

You can't buy that in a cheap bag of potting mix from a big box store. It takes a master gardener years to nurture and build a soil like that. If you buy "organic potting mix," the meaning of "organic" is the same as with the nutrients – organic provenance, no chemicals added. I've tried these formulations. There may be better brands. The ones I've tried are simply inferior to the basic cheap Miracle Gro potting mix. My plants don't like them. The organic potting mix is much more expensive – for inferior plant growth.

This may seem counter-intuitive, but if you want a more organic container project, I'd recommend shooting for the spirit of the thing. In terms of environmental impact, try a renewable inert substrate, like coco coir, preferably mixed with perlite, or growstones made from recycled glass, or even clean pebbles. Coco coir is just fiber from coconut husks, chemically neutral. It compacts well for shipping and storage, grows plants quite well, and provides no nutrients at all. Perlite qualifies as organic growing – it's a puffed volcanic glass. Then feed the plants with organic hydroponic nutrients.

Or simply use Miracle Gro potting mix – because it works – and an organic fertilizer. Most of my potted projects use that compromise.

Another place organic growing comes into all this, is in the seed itself. Organic seeds are simply grown on organic farms. The chemical load that a non-organic seed contributes to your food, is microscopic compared to the chemicals in your water supply. But buying organic seed supports organic farms.

And then there's *heirloom* seed, which means the seeds from your crops can be saved and grown again, to produce nearly the same variety of crop. *Hybrid* seeds – especially *F1 hybrids* – don't have that property. Hybrid seeds are produced by crossing parent stock that are dissimilar from the hybrid variety. The parent plant generally doesn't produce a desirable harvest itself, other than the hybrid seed. When you grow seed saved from hybrids, you get some other re-scrambling of this genetic material, not as good as the hybrid.

So why grow hybrids? They often provide predictable growth, higher yields, enhanced flavor or appearance qualities, and genetic disease resistance packages. Plant breeders develop these hybrids in the hope of generating profits, and develop robust varieties with lovely features. I'm all for preserving biodiversity and heirloom crop varieties. But in truth, we could not feed the current population of this planet without hybrid crops, hybrid rice in particular. Hybrids are not an evil plot, and hybrids are well worth growing. Granted, one of the corporations that sells hybrid seed – Monsanto – is not exactly on my Christmas gift list.

Hybrid carmen peppers, and heirloom mini red stuffing peppers, grown indoors.

Seed-saving is unlikely to save you significant money as an indoor gardener. The heirloom-vs-hybrid argument is really a political, environmental issue. I play it both ways, myself. I enjoy the yield and disease resistant features of growing hybrids. I also have one heirloom pepper variety I keep growing. I save the seeds, and share with anyone who wants them. It's a robust hybrid, producing carefree big crops indoors and out, a virtually indestructible plant that grows walnut-sized bell peppers. Pepper seeds are super easy to save – but they only keep for two years. So they have to be grown fairly often. I grow other heirlooms, too, without saving the seeds.

But I also grow hybrids, especially tomato hybrids. Tomato heirlooms are often plagued with disease, low yields, and slow time to maturity. I just don't have room for a giant plant that might or might not deliver fruit. But other gardeners won't grow anything but heirloom tomatoes, and insist the flavor of all hybrids is inferior.

One exciting new movement in the US is toward seed banks, sometimes in lending libraries. You can "check out" some heirloom seeds, grow them, and return the saved seeds from your crop. This may be worth a look if you have a seed bank in your area. Free seeds, and giving back to the gardening community, and preserving our diverse crop heritage.

Another issue you may hear about lately is genetically modified organisms, or GMOs. A hybrid is *not* the same thing as a GMO. Hybrids are the result of plant breeding, crossing two individuals of the same species, to get a superior child variety. This isn't greatly different from what your parents were up to when they made you, though perhaps more deliberate.

In truth, every plant we eat has been bred this way from wild types, to create varieties that serve humans better. In contrast, a GMO is the product of genetic engineering, splicing in genes from a different species. This is typically done on continental-scale crops like corn and soybeans, not our indoor salad crops. This is a risky business, and worth keeping an eye on. But it isn't really a concern for our purposes in this book.

So where does organic growing fit in your indoor salad growing? That's mostly a question of politics and conscience. On the pragmatic side – just make sure that whatever you choose, it's clean enough to share your home environment with. The more "natural" your ingredients, the easier it is to grow some truly appalling biology experiments, featuring disgusting, reeking slimes and molds. That's not healthy. Keep it clean. And clean it often.

Summing Up

The root zone provides nutrients, water, physical support, and air. The plant processes in the root zone may be hidden from view, but they're crucial to the success of your crops, just as your breath and heartbeat are crucial to your life.

Solutions in the root zone form a continuum, more than discrete choices. At one extreme, you put seed in dirt, water it, and hope for the best. This chapter described ways to improve on that formula with container growing. Then we introduced hydroponics and aeroponics, where we leave the dirt behind.

What's best? Whatever works for you.

As for the plants, there are some crops where deep water culture hydroponics works so poorly that you should stick to potting mix, or invest in more expensive hydroponics. Spinach and cucumbers fall in that camp. There are other plants where hydroponics gives such faster yields, that it would be a shame to use potting mix – lettuce and basil are prime examples. But for most of our salad crops, all of these technologies work well enough, with a little know-how.

I considered a DIY Root Zone chapter for this book, as with the DIY Grow Lights. But the tricks are specific to each plant group. So instead, each of the plant group chapters finishes up with a project.

Next up – grow lights.

Chapter 4
Grow Lights

Plants convert light into food energy, via photosynthesis. You know this at some level of scientific detail, depending on your interest in such things.

The energy on planet Earth, and the energy used to make all of our food supply, comes from the sun. The sun generates light by hydrogen fusion, a process you're not going to replicate in your living room. You know this, too.

The most costly part of growing plants indoors, both to our environment and your checkbook, is providing enough light. Well, you could spend more on a hydroponic rig for the root zone. But you'd still have to provide enough light somehow. To grow good crops under electric lights, the plants need light 12 to 16 hours a day, which can rack up quite a few kilowatt-hours on your power bill.

√ **Tip:** Use sunlight if you can. It's what the plants want, and it's free.

Sunlight also provides all the wavelengths of light that a plant uses. If you can provide even a couple hours of sun per day, the quality of your artificial lights for the rest of the day won't be as critical, and your plants can manage with fewer hours of light.

Do you need artificial lights at all? That depends on what you're growing, and how many hours of full sunny window are available. Most leafy crops can tolerate pretty low light – indirect sun for 6 hours a day would be enough for them. But they won't grow very quickly. Having light for 12 to 16 hours a day will grow more crop. The immature fruits need the same hours of light, but indirect sun is not enough. They need 4-plus hours of direct sun, plus light for a total of 12 to 16 hours per day. The mature fruiting plants need 6-plus hours of direct sun, plus light for the remainder of 12 to 16 hours per day.

Because life is perverse, the fruiting plants also require *dark* for 8 hours a day. Leafy plants are OK with it being light all the time. But some flowering plants won't flower without some dark time.

So in general, to grow crops indoors, at least some of the time you'll probably need artificial light to get good yields. If you don't, congratulations. By all means, skip on to the plant chapters. If you find you need more light later, these chapters will still be here.

The rest of us need to figure out how to spend some money wisely.

If you're putting artificial lights in a window, by the way, please note that these lights are *bright*, during some hours (at least in winter) when it's dark outside. This could cause some friction with the neighbors.

In the warmer months, you don't want direct sunlight in your house. Sunlight turns into heat. If the air conditioner is running, you might not save on your electric bill by using sun instead of artificial light.

Also, depending on how far north you are, even full direct sunlight might not be enough light in winter for the summer crops – cucumbers and tomatoes especially. And depending on your neighborhood, you might not want your curtains open all the time, or to keep opening and closing them.

In practice, most people growing indoor crops will need some artificial light, at least to grow crops in winter.

Fair warning – we talk tech in this chapter. If the discussion gets too deep for you, but you still need grow lights, not to worry. Chapter 5 presents some cheap and easy DIY light projects.

Timers

√ **Tip:** Lights need to be on a timer.

Your grows need light for 12-16 hours per day.

You can buy a plug-in timer for $10-$15 at a hardware or big box store. The cheapest timers are designed to turn a lamp on and off to discourage burglars by pretending someone's home. If you buy a new timer for the purpose of controlling grow lights, some features to look for include:

- A "heavy-duty" timer, with 3-prong grounded outlets.
- Two outlets, instead of one.
- Ability to set multiple on/off times per 24 hours.
- Preferably one that doesn't click all the time.

The nice thing about having a grounded, 3-prong outlet on the timer, is that you can plug a power strip into it. A surge protector also works as a power strip, though for ordinarily lights you don't really need the surge protection. (For HID lights – high intensity discharge – follow the manufacturer's directions.)

A power strip allows you to add more lights, or plug in other devices, such as a Kill-a-Watt meter to measure how much power the project is using, or an air pump to oxygenate nutrients. If a crop project gets some direct sunlight, you can save money by having the lights turn on in the morning, off for the sunny hours, and back on to finish the day.

Most mechanical timers do *click*, unfortunately.

So turning the lights on for the proper length of time was easy enough. But what kind of lights?

Light and Distance

In lighting plants economically, it's important to understand that light falls off with distance from the light source. Picture a balloon. Uninflated, the balloon is small and opaque in color – it's thick. As you blow it up, the balloon gets stretched and its walls become increasingly transparent – it's thin. The light strength at any distance from a lamp is like the thin balloon walls as the balloon is inflated. The same absolute total amount of light is available one inch from the light, as one foot from the light. But at one foot from the light, the same number of photons are spread over a much larger area.

In physics terms, we'd say that light intensity falls off as the square of distance from the light source. At double the distance, you have one quarter the light. At quadruple the distance, you have one sixteenth as much light.

The first obvious problem here is that your plant leaves are not arranged in a sphere around your light bulb. So you can increase the light falling on the plants, by positioning a reflector to bounce the light in the right direction.

√ **Tip:** Use reflectors to direct light onto the plants.

The simplest light-with-reflector is a spotlight. These bulbs come with a built-in parabolic mirror, to herd all the photons into traveling in pretty much the same direction.

Next simplest – you could use a regular CFL helix light bulb, with the parabolic reflector on the outside. (CFL stands for compact fluorescent lamp.) A desk lamp does this. You can also buy a light-socket-on-a-cord with an aluminum reflector and a clamp for attaching it to something. This item is called a *"clamp lamp."* Or, any straight-tube fluorescent light fixture has a reflector of some quality – it points the light down, anyway. The cheapest version of this sort of fluorescent light fixture is called a *"shop light"* and costs around $20.

The websites that cater to people growing crops-of-high-street-value have *lots* of high-end lamp reflectors to choose from. But please spend some more time in this chapter learning the basics first, and the cheaper options, before braving the menu of stratospheric prices.

In addition to putting a reflector on the lights, you can also surround the plants with a reflector, to keep light inside the volume you want lit, and out of your eyes. More on that in Chapter 5 on the DIY light projects.

So does all that light reflecting cure the light-falls-off-with-distance effect? Not really. In theory, a perfectly parabolic reflector should perfectly focus a perfect point source of light, traveling through a perfect vacuum. In the real world, of course, none of those conditions apply. By using reflectors, we reduce the fraction of completely wasted light. But the basic rule still holds – a plant twice as far from the lights is less brightly lit.

Why do I bring this up, before discussing how much light you need to grow crops? Because:

1. It depends on the type of plant.
2. It depends on how far the light is from the plant.
3. The size of the plant itself impacts how far the light is from the plant.

If all the light is coming from the same direction, the far end of the plant is farther from the light. If the plant is an 8 inch tall lettuce, that may not make much difference. If the plant is a 6 foot tall tomato [1.8 m], it makes a lot of difference.

The brute force solution for big plants is to use a really, really bright light. This has its downsides. Huge lights are expensive. Once bought, they're expensive to run. You need protective eye-wear to be anywhere near them. They'll bleach your carpet and furnishings. So you need to enclose the plants and the really big light to protect your eyes and home. But the lights are hot, to the point where they'll cook your plants unless you add cooling devices. Once enclosed, they also require an air circulation system.

I dislike this really big light solution. This whole expensive snowballing problem came from not having a bright enough light to reach the far side of the plant. But a plain 23 Watt (23 W) CFL light bulb is bright enough to grow any crop plant – any part of the plant that's close enough to it. So rather than make one light bright enough, I can surround the plant with smaller lights. This takes less electricity. Unfortunately it takes a lot more light sockets, and some ingenuity on how to mount the lights. And since the plant grows towards all the lights, there's a bit more pruning to keep the plants from touching the light bulbs. Some leaves get burnt.

Wait! you may cry. *Don't the lights have to be above the plant, like the Sun in the sky?* Yes, just like the sun in the sky, the lights should shine on the upper hemisphere of the plant. Not below the soil. The Sun is brightest at the zenith. But even at local high noon, that zenith isn't directly above you – well, perhaps two days a year, if you live in the tropics.

Plants just like light on the top side of their leaves. Most plants are capable of adjusting their leaves based on the direction of the light. I've experimented. Positioning lights around the plant works well.

√ **Tip:** Place lights close to the plant, without burning them.

We still have a lot of options these days when it comes to selecting lights. And not all artificial lights are good for growing plants.

Lighting Technology Overview

In the next few sections, we take a look at the available lighting technologies, and what matters to the plants. Aside from sunlight, the options are:

- Fluorescent Lights – the linear tubes
- CFLs – compact fluorescent lamps
- LEDs – light-emitting diodes
- HID – high intensity discharge, MH (metal halide) and HPS (high pressure sodium).

Executive summary: fluorescents are cheap and effective. They can get the job done for all salad plants. I recommend fluorescents for beginners. LEDs, including current Aerogardens, also work but cost more – and beware chintzy LEDs that don't work. HID lights are a hard-core investment, for dedicated grow rooms only.

Along the way we'll talk about what plants need from a light. Bottom line, more intense lights are needed to grow tomatoes and marijuana. You can grow tomatoes with any of these technologies, but only if you choose certain compact tomato varieties and put some ingenuity and investment into your light fixtures. The other salad vegetables don't need such intense light.

Before we get into the hardware, a word on light color.

Kelvin and Colors

First, an executive summary. Then we'll explore what it means. The executive summary is:

When buying fluorescent lights, you need primarily 6500K *("full spectrum daylight")* bulbs for vegetative growth. This is a cold, bluish white light. Optionally, you can add in a few 4100K *("cool white")* bulbs to encourage flowering and fruiting. The so-called "cool white" light is warmer (yellower) than "daylight." Never take away all the 6500K light – your crop plants will always do some vegetative growing.

The K stands for Kelvin – more on that peculiar unit in a moment.

What is going on here?

We'll deal with MH, HPS, and LED later. For now, let's concentrate on the fluorescent technologies.

Plants use light as an energy source. But plants are green. That means they reflect away green light – they don't use it. Well, OK, not all plants are green – red lettuce springs to mind, from our list of target crops. But chlorophyll is green, and that's the component of the plant that handles photosynthesis.

A red plant doesn't crave red light. It doesn't use red *or* green light.

Full spectrum white light contains all colors – light of all wavelengths. But what plants need most from that spectrum is blue and red. There is a photosynthetic response curve to different wavelengths of light – google it if you care. There is a broad peak close to 6500K, with another peak near 4100K.

A plant given only light of a single wavelength would not thrive. They use the whole spectrum, to some extent. But they use those wavelengths the most.

But 6500K is not a wavelength. Nor a color. Kelvin is a unit of *temperature,* and we'd better hope 6500K doesn't happen in our homes. White hot iron is only around 1370K. How temperature is used to express light color involves the physics of black body radiation – which I don't understand.

Suffice it to say that a "full spectrum" 6500K light bulb has all the wavelengths of white light, with special emphasis around the blue. Likewise, 4100K is shifted toward the red that plants like.

Neither light is really "blue" or "red," just bluish and yellower.

A 5000K bulb is also called *"daylight."* I've seen successful grows that use them. I would prefer 6500K in any technology, because I've seen evidence that it grows better. But 5000K is the bluest LED 'daylight' I've seen for sale.

Tomatoes are unusually fond of the color red. I've even added in 2700K bulbs *("soft white")* for them when coaxing more flowers to open. They seem to like it.

The 4100K / 2700K lights have an effect. Flowers open faster. Maybe fruit ripen faster. However you can grow all of your crops, to harvest, using nothing but 6500K full spectrum lights. The purveyors of fine $100 light bulbs may suggest otherwise. Their lights might indeed do a better job than a 6500K CFL that costs $5. But the 6500K light gets the job done.

Unlike fluorescent and LED lights, the high-intensity discharge (HID) lights don't come in a choice of designer colors. Metal halide (MH) light is a blue-white. High pressure sodium (HPS) light is a sulfurous yellow. You've probably seen both used in street lights. To grow flowering plants with the HIDs you need *both* – MH for vegetative growth, and HPS for flowering and maturity.

LED (light emitting diode) grow lights used to be lurid magenta, incorporating only red and blue LEDs. They've gotten better in recent years. Plants need full spectrum light.

For what it's worth, you can now get salon red light therapy for your skin. A similar red to the wavelength plants prefer, is also claimed to decrease wrinkles by increasing collagen and elastin production. They claim it helps with acne, eczema, cold sores, even skin cancer. Maybe growing plants indoors is good for your complexion as well as winter seasonal affective disorder (SAD).

And before you invest in a light meter? It wouldn't help. A consumer-grade light meter can only measure one wavelength (color) of light. They don't measure what plants use.

Fluorescent Lights

The least expensive grow lights are fluorescent. They're cheaper to buy initially. If used strategically, by keeping the lights close to the plants, they may be the cheapest to operate as well.

But when I started building my own grow rigs for indoors, I found I didn't know as much about them as I thought I did. There's a light switch, right? You plug light bulbs into a socket. And flick the switch. Not much to it, really.

Lack of understanding can leave us vulnerable to pushy sales pitches. We don't want to be vulnerable to pushy sales pitches.

So this section is an introduction to fluorescent lights.

Fluorescent 48" shoplight, with 6500K T8 tubes. This growlight cost less than $30.
Works great for 4 square feet of seedlings and small plants like lettuce.

As if the color temperature thing weren't mystifying enough, straight fluorescent lights are sold by length, in inches, and diameter – measured in eighths of an inch. So a fluorescent tube labeled "T8" is 8 ÷ 8 = 1 inch in diameter. The common sizes being sold now are T8, and T5. That means the tubes are 1" and 5/8" in diameter.

The diameter may be given in millimeters instead of eighth-inches. Hence T26 for T8, or T16 for T5.

A CFL light (compact fluorescent light) is basically a T2 or T5 tube coiled to approximate the shape of an incandescent light bulb.

The narrower tubes are newer and more efficient. They are also more expensive. T12 was developed in the 1930's, and is now obsolete. T8 was developed in the 1980s, and T5 around 2000. T8 is about 10% less efficient than T5, at the ideal operating temperature of each.

That caveat is important, because the most efficient operating temperature of a T8 tube is close to room temperature, while the efficiency peak for a T5 tube is about 95 degrees Fahrenheit (35C).

By efficiency, we mean lumens of light per watt of power. For the same hit to your electric bill, how much light your plants get.

At room temperature, for maximum efficiency, it's fine to operate T8 lamps as bare tubes. But T5 need to be enclosed in the light fixture, so they heat up their own environment, hopefully to their more efficient range around 95ºF. Otherwise you spend more money on a T5 system, but get a light that is no more efficient than the cheaper T8.

T5 is more expensive in two ways, then. The enclosed light fixture is more expensive. And the tubes are more expensive. T5 runs as much as 3 to 4 times as expensive, and is only about 10% more efficient at best. T5 use different lengths and pin / socket configurations and "electronic ballast", so a light fixture is either T8 or T5, not interchangeable.

Relative prices change over time.

To make matters even murkier, light output efficiencies are measured for the wavelengths of light human eyes see best. That's a wavelength that plants don't use much. In fact, it's about halfway between the two wavelength spans that plants prefer. Human beings see green really well.

The bottom line is that many people find that T8 are a better value for growing plants.

But wait! There's another wrinkle on the T5 business. There are also T5HO tubes on the market – T5, high output. T5VHO means T5, very high output. Both are less efficient than T5, meaning that they produce fewer lumens of light per watt of electric bill. But they are brighter per tube. So, with T5HO you get much more intense lights and pay for electricity accordingly. T5HO are sold for overhead-style grow lights, because they generate more intense light without the jump up to HID lights.

Now what was this "ballast" business about?

With the familiar incandescent light bulb, a light socket is a pretty simple device. It provides threads to screw the bulb into, and electrical leads. Screw in a bulb and the circuit is complete – power can flow. That's about it. Light happens because electric current flows through a filament. The filament gets hot and glows.

This is not the case with a fluorescent tube. Supplying AC current (wall power) directly to the tube, isn't how a fluorescent works. Instead it relies on a "ballast" to smooth out the electrical current. Older magnetic ballasts may hum a bit. Newer electrical ballasts hum less. In the familiar straight-tube fluorescent lights, this ballast is built into the fixture.

Familiar T8 light fixtures are the bare-tube T8 shop light, and the drop-ceiling T8 lights that pave the ceilings of stores and office buildings and schools. The most common T5 fixtures lurk under kitchen cabinets to light the counters, fully enclosed in plastic. T5 and T5HO are growing in popularity as the prices fall.

CFLs

CFLs – compact flourescent lamps – took the U.S. by storm, as the government gradually banned the sale of most incandescent light bulbs. The CFL technology can fit into existing light fixtures, and give equivalent light, using a quarter of the electricity. Originally pretty expensive, CFL prices were subsidized by the power companies for a while. But now they're inexpensive, and everywhere.

Early CFLs had rather ugly light, but the CFL manufacturers now offer a wide variety of designer colors. There are still a few specialty incandescent bulbs that are hard to find a CFL equivalent for. But that's a testament to just how deeply wedded we've become to our lighting technology in the past century. Every room has at least one light switch, and usually the closets and outdoor spaces as well.

Technologies we embrace so thoroughly into our lives have side effects. Incandescent bulbs generate so much waste heat that the children's toy Easy Bake Oven was invented. CFLs have the more interesting side property of being good for growing plants.

Well, you could grow plants with incandescent lights, too. They're just so bad at it that very few people ever did.

Most of my indoor salad growing projects have used linear fluorescent shoplights and CFLs. Only recently have LEDs become an effective alternative.

Where do CFLs fit into the fluorescent scheme of grow light technologies?

A CFL – compact fluorescent lamp – is a T5 or T2 linear fluorescent tube, coiled into a more bulb-shaped volume. You can also buy CFL spotlights. Those are the same coiled tube housed in a parabolic reflector to bounce light into a single direction instead of all directions.

Some CFLs have pins, and rely on an external ballast. But the more familiar household CFLs, built to screw into an incandescent lamp socket, have an electronic ballast packed on board. They're also available in candelabra (smaller) and mogul (bigger) socket sizes.

Since the ballast isn't part of the original straight fluorescent tubes, the lighting industry standardized on quoting efficiency – lumens per watt – counting only the tube. The power consumed by the ballast is omitted. So all fluorescents, including CFLs, use a few more watts to operate than their labels suggest. For instance, a 23W CFL generally draws 25W to 27W of power, according to my Kill-a-Watt meter.

All CFLs, by the way, contain mercury. Mercury is highly poisonous to the environment – and you. The expression "mad as a hatter" comes from hat makers being exposed to mercury in their work, and gradually going insane from the neurological damage.

If a CFL breaks, clean carefully. When disposing of CFLs, take them to a proper recycling center. Home Depot accepts used CFLs around here. Please, never toss a used CFL into the trash, for its mercury to leech out and poison fish, birds, and mammals. And right back up the food chain onto your supper plate. For you, your children, and all the rest of us to become mad as a hatter.

In related news, virtually all CFLs for sale in the United States are manufactured in China.

Fluorescent Wrap-Up

So do you need specialty grow lights, fluorescents designed specifically for growing plants?

No. These fine specialty products might grow plants better than standard fluorescent lights. They often claim special mixtures of phosphors to provide better light wavelengths formulated for plants. Some glow a strange lavender. I haven't tested all these claims, though I've tried some.

But friends and I have found that regular 6500K full spectrum fluorescent lights, alone, can grow all the indoor salad crops. And yes, that includes ripening tomatoes. (Tomatoes do flower better with 4100K in the mix, though, or even the warm 2700K.)

In the end, the best choice of shape or wattage, T5 or T8, HO or non-HO, CFL vs. straight-line bulbs, is determined more by geometry than technology.

The highest efficiency of all is to not use light that isn't needed. For smaller plants, use less light. I often use CFLs instead of the others simply because I can add more, take some away, and aim the light directly where it's needed. This makes CFLs more scalable than the fixed-size linear fluorescent fixtures.

A shopping tip – not all fluorescent manufacturers are created equal. I've bought many CFLs with lifespans rated at 10,000-plus hours. Some lasted less than 2,000 hours. In my experience, the cheapest brands are not worth their price. One brand I've had good luck with is Westinghouse. I'm sure there are others. My area has many big box stores and all the shopping possibilities of the Internet, and I've shopped hard. My best buy on light bulbs is a locally owned hardware store. Their prices are slightly higher for their cheapest stuff. Because they don't carry the inferior grade products that don't work. I love this about them. I can safely buy their cheapest stuff, and it works.

Fluorescents Age

One more thing about fluorescents before we turn to other lighting technologies. With time, they become less bright and change color. For use lighting a room, this doesn't matter. But after 6 months or so, turned on 16 hours a day as growlights, fluorescents wear out. Replacing old fluorescent tubes or CFLs with fresh ones will make your plants grow better. The difference is visible.

Chapter 5, DIY light projects, presents some easy fluorescent light projects to get you growing.

But there's a new game in town, starting to supplant the cheap fluorescent options – LEDs.

LED Lights

In the last few years, since the first edition of this book, LED technology has advanced to become a competent low-cost grow light option. LED lamps are now starting to chase CFLs off the store shelves. CFLs are becoming harder to buy, with fewer options, as LEDs gain in popularity.

LED stands for light emitting diode. LEDs require less power than fluorescents for the same lumen output. Each individual LED may not be very bright, so they're configured into "screens" of multiple LEDs to make a single grow light.

LEDs are naturally directional instead of round. For spotlights and growlights, you don't need a light fixture to aim them.

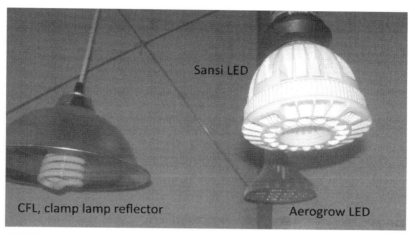

A CFL in a reflector vs. two LED growlights. See next picture for the plants.

Each LED diode can emit a different color of light. But newer diodes can also emit full spectrum light. And that makes all the difference for growing plants.

The promise of LEDs for growing plants is enticing – save energy by producing only the wavelengths of light the plants need. In theory, this ought to be way more efficient, shouldn't it? And LED manufacturers promise lifespans of LED lighting much longer than fluorescent tubes, which last a "mere" 10,000 operating hours.

With the early LED lights I bought to experiment with – cheap ones, admittedly – none of that promise was realized. I did several direct comparisons, growing with CFL and LED lamps of nearly the same wattage. These particular LED lights were *"tri-band,"* meaning they had white as well as red and blue LEDs. This made the light less obnoxious – slightly pink instead of lurid magenta.

But my plants grew better under 6500K fluorescent, period. And that promise of long life? Well, perhaps each individual LED would have lasted an eternity. But each little LED lamp is plugged into a screen, and the electronics of the screen failed within a month. It wasn't just me. Friends online tried the same experiments. All of us sent back our half-dead, failed-to-grow LED grow lights.

Whatever wavelengths of light plants use most, they need full spectrum light.

But 5 years later, now there are competent LED grow lights. Even Aerogarden systems are now sold with LED lighting panels instead of CFLs. I have two LED Aerogarden systems, and they grow salad crops fine. The LEDs last much longer than the 6 months before a fluorescent grow light should be replaced. And incorporating the "full spectrum" white lights, LED growlights are no longer lurid magenta.

That was a quick technology change!

I still can't find 6500K LED lamps, though. This concerned me. The LED "full spectrum daylight" bulbs are listed at 5000K. I tried a 5000K CFL spotlight once. I hung it over a cucumber vine trained horiztonally. The cucumber leaves bent away toward the nearest 6500K lamps instead of the 5000K light right above them. Cucumbers prefer 6500K.

So for this book revision, I tested LEDs again. I grew red and green lettuce under a 6500K CFL, versus in an LED Aerogarden, and against both an Aerogarden tri-band spotlight and a Sansi full spectrum LED (no red and blue lamps).

All lamps were competent to grow lettuce.

CFLs and T8s remain cheaper than LEDs in the short run. For this experiment, my 18 W CFL cost $5, vs. $20 for my 15 W Sansi full spectrum, and $25 for the 20 W Aerogarden spotlight. Fluorescent T8s for my shoplight cost $11 for two tubes at Home Depot. But they need to be replaced after 6 months of use.

You still need to shop carefully with LEDs. When I was selecting my Sansi lamp and the Aerogrow spotlight for my test, I still saw plenty of the same old drek out there for sale – cheap magenta lamps that would not grow plants well.

But with a little care, LEDs are a good growlight option now. And they'll continue to fall in price.

4-week red and green lettuce grown under the preceding CFL and LED lamps.

Front 2 plants are the same 4-week red and green lettuce in an LED Aerograden.

Aerogardens

The Aerogarden product line (Aerogrow, Inc.) combines timer, hydroponic base unit, and on-board grow lights. I love these, and have owned six of them. Many of us got turned on to indoor crop growing via Aerogardens, and banded together online to explore their possibilities and go beyond them. They're great products, though a bit pricey.

The Aerogarden is a turn-key system. Aerogrow guarantees your seed kit will grow, or they'll replace it. Aerogardens come with a choice of seed kit – herbs, salad greens, flowers, or cherry tomatoes, with more seed kits to choose from for future grows. Or you can grow your own seeds. The kits include hydroponic nutrients.

The Aerogarden is a great system for beginners. And they come in designer colors for the public rooms of your home.

Aerogarden continues to innovate. As of this writing, you can buy Aerogardens sized from a 2-plant system for children, on up to a "farm" system that can handle up to 24 plants. The farm has two nutrient reservoirs, so you could grow 12 lettuce and herbs on one side, while the other grows a few tomatoes and peppers. Aerogrow no longer sells CFL-based systems – all their newer systems use LEDs.

For this chapter, we're focused on lights. In addition to their turn-key systems, you can also buy Aerogarden LEDs in spotlight or screen form, independently of their all-in-one hydroponic systems. A 20 W Aerogrow LED spotlight is pictured in the LED section of this chapter.

The Aerogarden lights are good enough to grow all the salad crops. In my experience, and from seeing hundreds of other grows online, Aerogardens are bright enough and have the on-board space to grow herbs, salad greens, many flowers, jalapeño peppers, and dwarf eggplant.

A little extra help is needed to grow good tomatoes. Although Aerogrow sells tomato kits, and markets their systems for growing tomatoes, and they do in fact grow tomatoes – it is not a happy experience for most people. The Aerogarden just doesn't provide enough light. Starved for light, the tomato plants grow into the grow lights, and burn, so you prune them back. Alas, the flowers only form right there in the lights – the part you have to keep pruning back. If you have a tall Aerogarden model, you have physical room for more tomato plant, but there's still only enough light to bear fruit right up against the light. The result is a tall bare plant, that needs constant pruning to keep it out of the burning lights. Yields are low. To a lesser extent, the same problem occurs with large pepper varieties.

The answer is fairly simple. To grow tomatoes well in an Aerogarden, you need to add extra light. Putting the Aerogarden in a sunny window works. Or, add lights to the middle of the plant height, for a tall Aerogarden. Many people buy a crook-armed lamp with a sunlight bulb and point it at the middle of the plant. I devised a light screen for this, and experimented to find the right tomato varieties. DIY instructions for the lightscreen are in the next chapter.

The *"hydrophobic"* crops aren't happy in the Aerogarden's hydroponics. Lights aren't the problem.

Cherry tomatoes in Aerogarden with lightscreen (from rear).

HID Lights

HID stands for *"high intensity discharge."* The HID lighting technologies are metal halide (MH), which is a bright blue-white, and high pressure sodium (HPS), which is a deep yellow.

HID are the most efficient lighting technologies, in terms of lumens generated per watt. Most streetlamps use MH or HPS, though LEDs are gaining ground. Commercial winter greenhouses also use HID for supplemental lighting.

And I've never used them in my home. Why? Well, they're expensive. If you can believe the ad copy, you must also switch from MH to HPS as a plant matures from vegetative to fruiting stage. So to grow a tomato, you'd need both expensive technologies. There are convertible fixtures that can take either an MH or HPS bulb – but you still need both bulbs.

Unless you're growing tomatoes (or cucumbers, peppers, marijuana, etc.), you don't need this much light. And unfortunately, you don't need to buy just one of this expensive technology – it's a matter of both or neither.

Well, there are exceptions to that. HID is just overkill for lettuce and the greens, unless you're growing in commercial quantities. Vegetative lettuce doesn't require the redder HPS light, only the bluish MH light. Commercial greenhouses may also be able to skip either the MH or the HPS on fruiting plants, because their HID lights only serve to supplement sunlight.

Another problem with HID is that these lights run hot, and are damaging to eyes and furnishings. For a commercial greenhouse in winter, waste heat is a feature. In your living space, they can generate too much heat. This is where you get into those $500 "lighting" solutions, with light bulbs, fixtures, ballast, reflector, humidity control, air circulation system and thermostat to keep the plants from cooking.

I don't have a room in my house to convert to growing crops. I require my grow lights to politely co-habit space with human beings. That doesn't work with HID lights. They need to be enclosed away from living space.

I consulted briefly for a small commercial indoor crop venture, which used HID lights. They'd bought high-end 1000W lights for a little hot pepper plantation, thinking they were buying the very best. They would have done better to buy four lower-power light fixtures. The 1000W lights were too bright. Even hanging about 8 feet above the peppers, the poor young plants directly under them were scorched to death, with only the peripheral plants getting a survivable amount of light and heat. This wasn't the venture's only problem. They had no air conditioning, no fans, and ran these hot lights in an enclosed room in a summer warehouse. I felt so bad for them. The group spent thousands of dollars on deluxe HID lights and hydroponic systems. Probably ran up a big electric bill, too. They didn't harvest a single pepper.

HID lights can get great results. But I choose to leave them in the realm of commercial crop growers with staff to tend them. If you have the space, you might choose otherwise. If you're not experienced in growing crops indoors, though, I'd suggest that this technology is not for beginners. Or even intermediates.

This is a controversial conclusion among indoor growers.

Light – How Much is Enough

How much light is enough depends on the crop. Everything needs 12-16 hours of light overall. What varies is how strong the light needs to be.

Chapter 2 presented the relative light needs for the different types of crops. Greens are relatively low light. A fruiting plant needs more intense light – up to full direct sunlight. Tomatoes prefer at least 6 hours of direct full summer sunlight per day. More like 8 hours for the giant beefsteak type tomatoes.

Here are some rough guidelines, based on my own experiments. Provided the light is kept very close to the plants, a simple 2-tube T8 fluorescent light fixture with full spectrum 6500K lamps, can successfully grow any low-light plant that fits within about 10" below the light tubes [25 cm]. This 10" doesn't include the root zone, just the green part of the plant. The bright-enough footprint of that 2-tube lit volume is maybe 15" wide [30 cm]. If you wanted a wider footprint, you could add a second 2-lamp T8 light fixture, or use a 4-lamp fixture.

Plants that fit the bill include all salad greens, radishes, and all young plants intended for transplant to brighter light or the garden. That includes young tomato, pepper, and cucumber plants. Mixing plants is a bit of a challenge, if the root zone pots or whatever make the plants different heights.

If the green part of the plant is more than about 10" tall [25 cm], it won't get enough light. Fortunately, it's safe for plants to grow into the lights in a T8 system. The lights aren't hot enough to burn the leaves, although leaves on the lights will block the light from reaching anything below.

A simple 4-foot 2-bulb T8 shop light uses 64W of electricity to operate the light tubes, plus whatever the on-board ballast consumes. Over the course of a month, if the lights are on 14 hours a day, and power costs 15 cents per kWh, that should add about $4.25 on your electric bill – about the same cost as two bags of supermarket lettuce.

A T5 system changes the equation somewhat, because the T5s are brighter, smaller, more intense, and hotter. I haven't experimented with these much, but I believe the net result comes out about the same, except that the T5 lights need to stay at least 2" away from the still-10" plants. Somewhat brighter lights, but farther away, cancels out them being brighter.

Neither T8 nor T5 linear lights are intense enough for fruiting plants when they grow toward flowering size. For that, you need either T5HO lights, CFLs, or very short plants. I prefer CFLs because they can surround the plant, keeping most of the foliage within 12" of intense light. In this configuration, I've successfully grown full-size tomatoes on a perhaps 2.5 foot tall plant [75 cm] with eight 23W CFL light bulbs – less than 200 watts. To use fewer bulbs, the lights would be farther from the foliage on average. The same compact tomato might take a 250W CFL, or equivalent T5HO lights, if all the light came from fixtures above the plants.

Full size peppers take less light. Two or more plants can physically fit in the same brightly lit grow volume, with only six CFLs. Vining cucumbers are less dense, but bigger. Two plants can fit in a bit larger volume, and produce nicely with only 150W of distributed CFLs, or linear T5HO lights. I haven't experimented as much with beans and peas, but I would expect them to have similar light requirements to cucumbers.

How can you tell that your plants have enough light?

Plants have a limited playbook for solving problems. If they don't have enough light, they stretch to seek more. Young plants and vegetative vegetables get "leggy" with too little light. They stretch, with too much stem between leaves. (But note that when a mature lettuce does this, it may also be *"bolting"* – the end of its useful life cycle.) On the underside of the plant, leaves that don't get enough light will yellow and die.

If you happen to be growing red lettuce, it only grows red under enough light. Under too little light, mature leaves stay pale green with freckles. (Young leaves are always green-with-freckles.) You can use this as a light meter of sorts – if the red lettuce is bright red, you've got bright enough light for any greens.

Radishes fail to plump up their roots under too little light. Radishes grow quickly (~30 days), making them a useful diagnostic crop.

Mature fruiting vegetables show that they're not getting enough light by their shaded leaves turning yellow, and by aggressively growing into the lights. Stems farther from the grow lights become bare as yellowed leaves fall off. Fruit don't seem to finish ripening (tomatoes), or fall off (peppers), or shrivel (cucumbers). Or there simply aren't many flowers or fruits.

Even if you choose a different main lighting strategy, like linear shop lights or LEDs, you can add CFLs closer to the plants to supplement the main light, as needed. And use reflectors, to help the plants make the most of whatever light you provide.

If plants get too much light, or heat, the leaves closest to the lights burn, grow dry and brittle, or otherwise die. The leaves may wilt and droop. Flowers drop off without setting fruit.

On tomatoes and peppers, ripening fruits can get sun scald from too much light. Sun scald is a white or tan dead patch on a light-facing side of the fruit. Sun scald and "blossom end rot" look similar. If the blemish is on the end of the fruit where the blossom fell off, it's more likely to be blossom end rot than sun scald.

Summing Up

For indoor crop growing, we have many lighting technologies to choose from. Each has pros and cons. The easiest to work with for beginners are the fluorescent light technologies, but even there you have a lot of choice.

The simplest solution? Use 6500K daylight CFL bulbs. And use reflectors to point the light at the plant. For fruiting plants, begin adding 4100K cool white CFL bulbs when they begin to flower, transitioning to a mix of 6500K and 4100K lights.

Chapter 5, on DIY light projects, presents some simple and inexpensive grow light projects.

Indoor Salad

Chapter 5
DIY Grow Light Projects

This chapter presents some simple do-it-yourself projects for building your own home grow light rigs. The projects are based on fluorescent lights, though you may find ideas to adapt to HID or LED lighting projects. The projects are:

- Reflectors
- Lettuce and seedling shelf
- Crop pen
- Aerogarden surround

These grow light projects can be functional bare-bones, or beautifully finished to complement your décor. That's up to you. You can also mix and match any root zone solution you wish with these lighting systems. Chapter 3 covers root zone options.

Project: Reflectors

Chapter 4 mentions two kinds of reflectors. A reflector on the light fixture serves to direct light in one direction – toward the plants – instead of expanding out in a sphere. You can also put reflectors around the plants, to bounce light back onto the plants at the receiving end, instead of allowing wasted light to scatter into the room, or into your eyes.

In these projects, we surround the plant growing volume with reflectors, to keep the light on the plants, and limit spillover into our rooms and eyes.

Reflectors are useful for sunlight as well as growlights. For instance, if I have a pepper plant by a sliding glass door, I can put a reflector behind it to capture more sun and direct it at the back side of the plant. The reflector also helps keep the hot sun out of my room.

People often think "metallic" is the best reflector. Maybe that's because mirrors reflect, and they're metallic. But actually, white reflects light best. Picture a mirror hung on a white wall. The wall is usually brighter than the mirror, yes? White diffuses light instead of focusing it. At the source light fixture, you want light focused toward the plants. So light fixture reflectors often use mirrored surfaces. But on the receiving end, we want light diffused back onto the plants.

I've made simple surround-type reflectors out of:

- Emergency thermal blanket
- Tri-fold presentation board
- Sheets of foam-core board
- Coroplast
- Light-colored walls (for the back side)

Shrink-wrapped tri-fold presentation boards, foam core
board, and coroplast sheets in front.

Placing a grow project with its back to a white wall or corner can reduce how much material you need for an enclosure. Opaque materials in front glow attractively with lights inside, without allowing much light to spill out into the room or sear your eyes.

White foam core board (including tri-fold presentation board) glows golden with bright lights behind it. I often find foam core board products at a discount at job lot stores (Big Lots, Ocean State Job Lots), or at an office supply or craft store for full price (Staples, Michaels). Foam core board is opaque – its glow won't bother your eyes. You can cut foam core board with a utility blade (X-acto knife, etc.), along a steel straight-edge.

Coroplast is corrugated plastic, a hollow extruded plastic with ribs, or "flutes." It comes in various thicknesses, with the most common 4 mm (5/32 of an inch). In cross-section, that would be a line of 4 mm square cells. With lights behind it, white coroplast glows with a cooler, bluer version of whatever color light is behind it. You can cut coroplast with a utility knife, just as with foam core board. There's also an inexpensive tool called a "coro-claw" for cutting coroplast along its flutes, as quick as pulling a zipper. Coroplast is not generally available at retail stores. Sign makers have it, usually in 4 foot by 8 foot sheets. For few dollars per cut, the sign maker will likely be willing to cut the coroplast sheets for you across the grain, into more manageable pieces. He may also have a coro-claw for cutting along the grain.

Coroplast is less opaque than foam core board. If a light bulb is close to the coroplast wall, it's a bit hard on the eyes.

An emergency thermal blanket is mirrored like mylar, not white. But it's cheap, and convenient to drape as a curtain entrance on a plant enclosure. You can dimly see the plants through it. Best of all, I bought one emergency blanket for less than $2 a few years ago, and still haven't used all of it. An emergency blanket can cover a lot of area for very little money. Because they're semi-transparent, they won't protect your eyes as much from intense lights.

Many indoor growers also buy mirrored mylar or special matte white plastic sheeting for enclosure-type reflectors. Those would be more expensive. But their strength and flexibility would be easier to work with for building a grow tent. For instance, if you wanted to build a tent frame out of plastic PVC pipe, and then clip sides onto the frame, mylar or white sheeting would drape around the pipes.

PVC pipe is a fun building material itself, by the way, for those without access to a wood shop, or with limited woodworking skills. With many connector joints available, the material is like tinker toys for grown-ups. Hardware stores carry PVC pipe and the more common connectors, and may be willing to cut it to whatever lengths you need. PVC may be recyclable in your area – check earth911.com online.

Regardless of what you're using to enclose your grow volume, the plants need air circulation. So don't completely seal off an enclosure, unless you're prepared to add air vents and fans, etc. Leave it open for air flow.

Project: Lettuce and Seedling Shelf

This is my most useful all-around grow light rig, suitable for early growth of any plant, flowers and vegetables for transplant, or full life cycle leafy greens. For this, we use inexpensive shop lights, suspended from hooks and chains. We need the light tubes within 10 inches of the plants, so suspending the lights from the ceiling is not very convenient. Instead, I suspended the lights from a plastic utility shelf.

This is the same grow rig that appeared in Chapter 4, Fluorescent Lights, detached from the rest of the shelving and placed on a water-friendly tile hearth.

Pansy seedlings in lettuce and seedling shelf, using 2 x 32W T8 shoplight.

Parts:

- 48" long, 2-tube T8 fluorescent shop light fixture – around $20.
- Two 6500K 32W T8 bulbs to fit the shop light - $10.
- One shelf of plastic storage shelves (18"x36"x55") - $20 for a 4-shelf unit.
- Emergency thermal blanket - $2.
- Electrical timer - $15.
- A few nails for light height adjustment.
- Tape.
- Optional flooring – plant trays, seedling heat mat, waterproofing, etc.

Take one 18" high section of the stacking utility shelves, with its legs, and place it on a 48" x 18" waterproof bit of floor or table.

Utility shelves are perforated with drainage and air circulation holes. Find some nails long enough to reliably span the holes. Thread one of the shop light chains up through a hole, and spear the chain with two nails. The shop light essentially hangs from the nails, with the nails supported by the utility shelf. Repeat for the second shop light chain, assuming your shop light is suspended from 2 chains.

Insert the T8 lamps into the shop light. Plug the shop light into the timer and set the timer for 14 hours a day, to coincide with any times of day that the room is normally lit. Plug the timer into the wall, and make sure the shop light is turned on. The timer will turn it off.

Warning: Beware of water and electricity.

When plugging in anything around plants, the electrical cord should be arranged to dip below the electrical outlet. Then when water spills, the water follows the electrical cord down to its lowest point, and drips down from there. Make sure that lowest point is not your power outlet.

Adjust the height of the lights so that the T8 lamps are 2" from the tops of the plants [5 cm]. Or 6" is fine for germinating seeds [15 cm]. (Yes, some seeds require light to germinate, including lettuce.) For multiple height plants, it's OK to have the shop light fixture tilted at an angle, with the plants arranged from shortest to tallest.

Cut two rectangular pieces out of the emergency blanket, about 18" by 36". Tape them at the top to form drapes on the two long sides of the shelf unit.

That's it – you now have a growing area. If the seedling shelf is on the floor, you should have about a 15"x48" usable footprint, about 14" high at most. [In metric, that's a 38 x 120 cm footprint, 35 cm high.]

Variations

There are plenty of variations on this simple scheme. The utility shelves were simply something to suspend the lights from, with enough height below for the plants. A four foot long table-like structure, or swing-set A-frame shaped structure would do that just as well. There are also more attractive wooden utility shelves.

Or, you could simply hang the shop light from the ceiling with long chains.

Two T8 bulbs aren't painfully bright to look at, so the emergency blanket is an optional nice touch – you could skip it.

These shelves are stackable. But I'm leery of water leaking down from one layer of plants into another light fixture below. Unless you have a high-confidence solution to the water problem, I wouldn't recommend stacking shop lights. But you can place a single light shelf on top of the other shelves to keep the plants at a more convenient height for viewing and tending, and stow water-tolerant paraphernalia beneath.

There's a limit to how wide a shop light fixture you can fit between the legs of a utility shelf, but you might be able to squeeze in a 4-tube 128W fixture for twice the light. That would yield enough light and volume to grow one or two cucumber vines, with the pot placed beyond the end of the shop light. The vines could clamber along the floor under the lights.

With just the two T8 lamps, the light shelf provides enough light and height to grow leafy greens.

This grow rig has its limitations. For one, it's all-on or all-off. When my seedling shelf is in use, it consumes nearly a kilowatt-hour of electricity per day, with no way to reduce its power consumption when I have fewer plants. So my seedling shelf is turned on in January to start pansy seedlings, and usually turned off in May when my last summer transplants move outdoors. During those months, I may tuck other crops in around the transplants, a quick tub of radishes here, a little hydroponic lettuce there. But I grow a lot of outdoor transplants – flowers, tomatoes, peppers, eggplant, herbs, lettuce – so the shelf is kept pretty busy from January to May.

I keep my shelf in the coolest room in my house, because baby pansies and the other spring transplants require that. I add a seedling heat mat on one side for the heat-loving summer seedlings. Tomatoes and peppers especially take much longer to germinate under cool conditions.

Project: Crop Pen

The crop pen is a simple white surround, with CFL lights hanging around the plant, to keep most of the leaves brightly lit. This is suitable for mid-size fruiting plants, such as dwarf tomatoes, peppers, and cucumbers.

There are many ways to build a crop pen. But I started with this sort.

Carmen pepper in a crop pen made from tri-fold presentation board.
A dowel rests on the board to suspend the lights from.

71

Indoor Salad

Parts:

- Two tri-fold presentation boards, white foam core, 48"x36" – $10 - $30.
- 36" wooden dowel, about 5/8" thick. Can cut to 30" if desired. Around $2.
- 4 hanging lamp sockets. I buy these for $5 apiece from IKEA - $20.
- Electrical timer - $15.
- Power strip or surge protector – providing 4 to 8 power sockets.
- Two 6500K CFL spotlights (built-in reflector), 23W to 26W, about $18.
- Two 4100K CFL helix bulbs (no reflector), 23W – about $10.
- (Optional) Self-watering planter, about 14" diameter, 11" tall – about $10.

To put this together, cut notches at the top of the short sides of a tri-fold presentation board, for the dowel. Position the notches about 2/3 of the way out the short sides – so, 4 inches from the free edge of the 12 inch sides. Rest the dowel across the notches on the standing tri-fold board.

Suspend the hanging light sockets from the dowel, using twist-ties to adjust their height. The spotlights go in the middle, sending light down on the top of the plant. Cheaper helix bulbs can hang lower at the sides to provide light to the sides of the plant. There's no need to plug in all of these lights until the plant is big enough to need the light – a single overhead bulb is bright enough until the seedling is 10" tall. Add the 4100K bulbs last, when the plant starts to flower.

Set the timer for 14 hours a day and plug it into the wall. Plug the power strip or surge protector into the timer. Plug the lamp cords into the power strip.

The second tri-fold presentation board simply wraps around the first, to enclose the pen. It's awkward to move the presentation board that supports the lights. And you want to make it as convenient as possible to tend your plant daily. Of course, you could use something other than a tri-fold presentation board to close off the front. But you do want to close off the front – those bright lights are good for the plant, hard on the eyes. Should you want to expand your pen, the second tri-fold board could support a second dowel and light collection.

Arrange some waterproof material under the pen to protect the floor – a white trash bag works. Fill your self-watering planter with potting mix, add water to the reservoir, plug in some seeds, or transplant in a seedling. You could also use a hydroponic root zone solution instead of a potting mix container.

This particular pen is suitable for one average-sized pepper plant. Adjusting the geometry a bit, two smaller pepper plants could fit in it, using smaller pots, possibly with all spotlights instead of two helix bulbs. Or, the pen could fit a dwarf tomato or eggplant.

This is a flexible little crop pen. Its biggest drawback is its height. Though 36" is taller than most plants need to be, much of the headroom is lost to container height, lamp sockets, and large spotlights. Even in the picture above, I added a bit of styrofoam at the top to raise the dowel a couple inches.

Frustrated by this headroom limit, I later made a superstructure out of PVC pipe to hang the light sockets from. This works. Then, the tri-fold presentation board just acts as a reflector, keeping the light in the pen. Later I set the PVC pipes to dangle lights by a window, with some winter cucumbers between the flattened-out reflector board and the western sun. The lamps and reflector augmented the free but thin winter sunlight.

PVC light bar, with pepper plant. The tri-fold reflector rested
on the planter, when closed.

Projects in chapters 7 and 8 present variations on this crop pen more suited to cucumbers and compact tomatoes.

Project: Aerogarden Light Boosters

If you have an Aerogarden, most likely your plants' growth is light-limited. This may be less true if you only grow the lower-light greens and herbs. But generally speaking, if you grow anything that requires that the Aerogarden lights be raised from their lowest positions, you could get better growth by giving the plants more light.

For lettuce and herbs, this is merely a nicety – better yields. But the more light-demanding the plant, the more desperately they need the help. Good tomatoes especially may need more light than they can get from the Aerogarden's on-board lights. In online communities, we see this lament all the time. Someone wants tomatoes, they grow them in the Aerogarden, and virtually every flower grows right into the lights, needing to be pruned off. And no matter how often they prune, the tomato grows right back into the lights again. And no matter how tall the Aerogarden is, the plant doesn't seem to grow fruit in any of the extra volume below the lights.

The tomato plant simply needs more light.

So, to get better growth out of your Aerogarden, you can:

- Get more mileage from the Aerogarden lights by adding a surround reflector.
- Add lights.
- Add both.

To grow full-size tomatoes in an Aerogarden, you really need both. Or, a sunny spot to place the Aerogarden.

Aerogarden Mirror Wrap

The simplest, cheapest thing you can do to boost your Aerogarden lights, is add a surround-type reflector. A bonus on this is that it keeps the Aerogarden lights out of your eyes. The lights are certainly bright enough to make that a Good Thing. Aerogrow itself sells a solution for this, called a Power-Grow Light Booster. My solution came along before theirs, and allows you to see your plants better.

- Emergency thermal blanket - $2.
- Tape.

Before deciding how to add some blanket to the Aerogarden, it's important to understand that the plants need air circulation. You also need to tend your plants. Fortunately, a thermal blanket is large and cheap, so you can easily experiment and revise your craftsmanship. But note that tomatoes and peppers like it warm, and greens like it cool. The blanket helps with the former. It's a problem with the latter. Lettuce kept too warm will bolt – get long and straggly and go to seed.

So, for a lettuce Aerogarden, or flowers (which I simply want to see better), I add only a visor to the Aerogarden. Cut a strip of mirrored blanket about 3 inches wide, and long enough to go around most of the perimeter of your Aerogarden light hood. Tape it in place, as a short visor drape. Most of the light escaping from the hood is mirrored back onto your plants, and the lights stay out of your eyes. And this visor is short enough that it doesn't interfere with plant visibility. The tips of your lettuce get a little warm, but that won't make the plant react to the warmth by bolting.

Aerogarden minis with partial visor drapes, allowing for air and light to shine between them. Lettuce left, coleus and snapdragons right, with manual-hydroponic komatsuna in between.

For a warm-weather bright-light plant, you can use a longer drape. But the plant still needs plenty of air circulation, and you still need access to your plant. So for this, cut four rectangles of blanket. The newer Aerogarden hoods are rectangular. You'd want narrower drapes for the ends, and wider drapes for the length. Keep about a 2 inch gap between adjacent drapes. For length, cut the drapes so that the back and sides (at least) are as long as the Aerogarden is tall at max extension. Or, it's perfectly OK to make the drapes only long enough to reach the base of the Aerogarden when the light hood is at its lowest. Tape the four rectangles to the light hood, as before, leaving that crucial 2 inch gap between drapes. Tape the front really well, because you'll be flipping that back and forth to tend your plants.

You can see your plants through the thermal blanket drapes, dimly. And they'll love the extra light they're keeping.

Aerogarden Surround

Another reflector approach is to add a white surround, as with the crop pens. The easiest one:

- One tri-fold presentation board, white foam core, 48"x36" – around $15.

Simply place the presentation board around the front of the Aerogarden. Remove it to tend the plant.

I prefer to see my plants all the time, so I would cut the board down to 26" tall instead of 36" tall, for a tall Aerogarden. That takes a steel straight-edge and a utility knife – X-acto knife or similar. Cutting foam core board takes patience. I recommend practicing by cutting the first 6" off. When you have the knack of making a nice cut, then cut the board to the final height you want. In general, use a fresh sharp blade, go slow, and cut in multiple passes, never pressing too hard.

Foam core board with bright light behind it, glows a nice yellowish, so this looks nice. And the reflector gives your larger plants much more air circulation and grow volume than the mirrored drape approach does. With just this surround alone, no additional lights, you can quickly see young tomato plants change shape. Instead of reaching hungrily for only the lights, they start to spread out sideways towards the light of the walls.

Be careful of plants resting on the surround, though. That's great for supporting heavily laden plants – until you remove the surround. Make sure the stems are supported by something else well enough that the plants don't flop over and break their stems when the surround is removed. I lost a delicious full-sized tomato plant that way in its productive prime.

Project: Aerogarden Lightscreen

This solution is harder to make. I've grown a lot of delicious tomatoes with it!

IndoorSalad CropLampSurround, growing beefsteak tomatoes.

The idea here is to combine a simple white surround, as in the preceding project, with on-board lights. So that the middle of the plant gets not merely light reflected from the Aerogarden light hood, but more light. The surround acts as a reflector for these extra lights, as well as the Aerogarden lights. This solution gives enough light to grow even full-size beefsteak tomatoes in an Aerogarden – for a very compact variety of tomato plant.

Conceptually, there's nothing difficult to this – I add a few shelves to the surround. The top flange-shelves are for decoration, and to keep light reflected down into the middle of the plants. The lower flat shelves support the lights. The hard parts are:

Indoor Salad

1. Cutting the surround, and
2. Attaching the lights.

Also, if you put this much work into your surround, wouldn't it be nice if it were waterproof? And washable?

Alas, although tri-fold presentation board is easy to buy, works great, and its antique warm glow looks lovely – the board is clad in white paper. It's not waterproof. A tomato plant can live 6 to 9 months for a productive grow. Spills happen. The paper wrapping on the board wicks up water and starts looking diseased at the bottom.

So for this, I use coroplast.

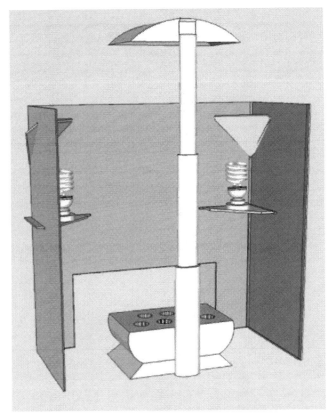

Schematic of IndoorSalad CropLampSurround, from rear.

Parts:

- White coroplast sheet, cut to 48"x26". The flutes are 26" long. Cost $5-$20.
- Electrical timer - $15.
- Power strip or surge protector – providing at least two power sockets.
- Two CFL helix bulbs, 23W, 6500K – about $10.
- *Either* two IKEA Hemma hanging lamp cord sets – about $10,
- *Or*, two standard flat-mounting lamp sockets, about 10' of lamp wire, a plug, and electrical connectors.

The first step is to cut a tri-fold presentation board, 26" high, out of coroplast. There are special tools to do this, and it's highly unlikely you own them. But your local sign maker does. So I recommend you negotiate with your sign maker to do the first cuts for you. You want him to cut a 26" strip off the end of a standard 4'x8' sheet of coroplast. And also, ask him to cut the coroplast strip *halfway* through at the 12" and 36" wales, for the two short sides of the tri-fold. Actually, make it about 11 3/4" and 36 1/4", so that the tri-fold can fold flat for storage, without the short sides overlapping. A sign maker typically has a giant cutter for slicing coroplast sheets perpendicular across the grain, and a small tool called a coro-claw that can zip through the half-cuts in a matter of seconds. Bring the picture with you, to explain what you're building.

If the sign maker is amused enough to offer to do all the cuts for you, take him up on that offer! The remaining cuts are hard to do.

Assuming the sign maker didn't do all the work for you, let's cut the rest of this. First, if the sign maker didn't do the half-cuts for you (you don't have a tri-fold yet, just a 48"x26" rectangle), start by deciding which side of your material is up, and forward. Set your utility blade to its shortest setting, so that it will only cut one face of the coroplast. Find the flute 12" from one edge, on the front, and move outward to halfway between two flutes, just under 12" from the edge. Use a steel straight-edge to cut down the middle between flutes, only 1 layer of plastic, 26" long from top to bottom. Repeat on the other side. Bend the sides and sit the tri-fold up, to make sure the half cuts are complete.

Before cutting any of the through-cuts, make sure you're working on a protected surface that won't destroy your utility blade. Putting foam-core board under the coroplast works.

Next, cut slots for the shelves to slide into. For these slots, you'll cut through the folded tri-fold – through 4 layers of flat plastic plus across the flutes. Draw all the cuts in pencil on the front of the folded board first. The lower slots are 15" up from the bottom, 6" across (horizontal, perpendicular to the flutes), and 4mm wide (for a 4mm thick shelf). To place the upper slots, measure 6" down from the top folded corner, and 6" across. Draw a solid line from the the bottom folded edge toward the other 6" mark, but only 6" long. Draw another line 4mm below it for the other side of the slot, for each slot.

Pause and inspect your pencil-drawn lines, to make sure it's all symmetric. Then cut, against a steel straight edge. Even with a very sharp new blade, it takes multiple passes to cut through all those layers of plastic.

Parts for the IndoorSalad CropLampSurround, screen folded in half for shipping.
I don't make these kits for sale anymore.

To verify your slots are cut well enough, set the tri-fold up, and slide the shelves in. A tight fit is better than a loose fit, but the shelves do need to slide in and out.

Next, cut an 8"x16" rectangle from the center bottom of the 24" side of your tri-fold. These cuts go through one layer of coroplast, not two. The hole is an access port to the Aerogarden base. Neatness counts.

Cut the removed 8"x16" rectangle into 4 triangular shelves. First cut it in half, into two 8"x8" squares. Then cut the squares on the diagonal to make 4 triangles. Then cut the acute angles off the triangles, about 2" in and parallel to the still-square corner. You could leave the acute corners if you prefer.

Next you need to attach lamp sockets to the two lower shelves. If you're using your own lamp sockets and wiring, I leave you to your own invention as to how to put it together – just be careful to ensure water can't follow the cords into the plug.

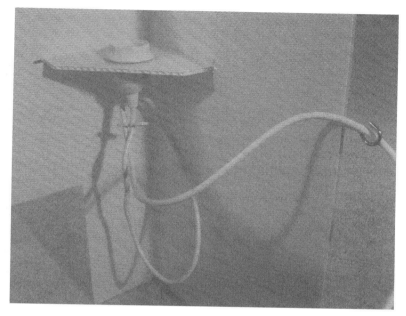

Wire management.

If instead you're using IKEA or other hanging lantern sockets, they should have a screw-on collar on the lamp socket. We attach the socket to a lower lightscreen shelf using that screw-on collar. So cut a hole in each of the two lower shelves, for the lantern socket (without collar) to push through. Use the screw-on collar to firmly attach socket to shelf. Push the shelf into its slot, sticking out ½" or so on the outside of the surround. The IKEA cord sets come with an eye hook and plastic wire-to-wire clamps. If you don't have those, make do with twist-ties and push pins, referring to the picture above. Your solution may vary. But the wire management needs to keep torque from tilting the light bulbs into the sides. So, I wrap the cord around under the shelf, to make it heavy, and keep the cord from pulling toward the back. I screw the eye-hook into the back edge as a wire guide (so that it sticks straight out the back, not through the wall). We also need a low point inside the surround, so spilled water doesn't travel down the cord to the power outlet.

Congratulations – your lightscreen is built. Plug it into the power strip / timer, and time the lights to come on during the same hours as the Aerogarden. It doesn't need to be exact. If the Aerogarden lights are on 16 hours a day, and the lightscreen is on some 12 hours of those 16, that's great.

Summing Up

In this chapter we looked at designs for some do-it-yourself grow light setups that cost greatly less than the sort of HID lighting and grow tent packages you'll find sold online. With these light rigs and variations on them, you have the light to grow any of the indoor salad crops. How well they fit your décor is up to your own craftsmanship. At significantly greater expense, you could replace the fluorescent lights with LED or HID lights, if desired. The principles are the same.

Next up – growing lettuce and greens!

Chapter 6
Leafy Vegetables
Lettuce, Greens, and Herbs

Leafy greens and herbs are probably the most rewarding crops to grow indoors. They grow fast. They're easy. They cost less to grow than to buy. And they're useful.

Almost any sandwich or meal can be improved with some fresh lettuce. Fresh-picked lettuce has more nutrients than aging supermarket lettuce, or even lettuce from the farm market. Aerogrow, the makers of Aerogarden, claim fresh-picked lettuce has up to 4 times the level of nutrients as store-bought. Around here, most of the winter supermarket lettuce is grown in California, on irrigated arid land, then trucked in across the continent, at substantial environmental cost. By the time you eat it, it may be a week old. In the fridge, it doesn't stay fresh much longer. The world throws out vast quantities of spoiled food each year, including slimy lettuce. Contrast that waste with simply having a few fresh, delicious, nutrient-packed lettuce leaves to add to your sandwich, any time. Whatever kind of lettuce you like – there's a wide variety beyond iceberg. Red and green, loose-leaf and crisp, substantial romaines, baby leaf, smooth and savoy and curly, rounded and oak-leafed.

Increasingly, people are going beyond lettuce for their greens, too. Mesclun mixes add "brassicas" – members of the cabbage family. Mustard greens, kale, Asian greens like pak choi, tatsoi, mizuna, and the horseradish-flavored komatsuna, are all popular additions to salads and sandwiches. Kale is lately a cult hit all of its own, used as a staple in health food smoothies, salads, and new variations on cooked dishes, in addition to its traditional role in minestrone.

Spinach and gaudy-stemmed dark chards, endive and radicchio, mache and amaranth, are all leafy greens outside the lettuce and brassica families. Radishes are grown the same way as leafy greens, too, though most people just eat the root. Bull's blood beet is grown for its dark red-purple leaves more than its root, although it can develop a respectable sweet round beet as well.

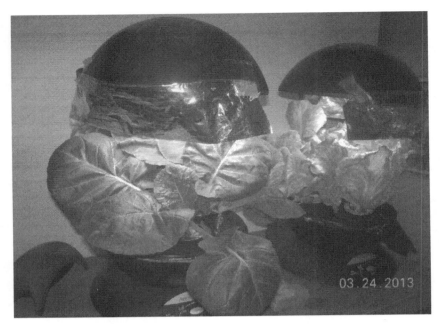

4-week senposai (a brassica) and 8-week summer crisp lettuce, in small Aerogardens.

If you use fresh herbs at all in your cooking, growing your own is cheaper. Fresh herbs are pricey. It's also awkward to plan ahead with herbs. Grow them yourself to simply have them on hand to add a little something to a dish. Snipped basil, dill, and parsley do wonders to freshen up canned soup.

I've grown most of these indoors, and they're easy. I don't grow all of them all the time, and most people won't. We keep growing what we get the most use out of. I grow lettuce indoors most of the time. Including during the outdoor growing months. The weather or bugs make outdoor lettuce problematic here for all but two months of the year. During the "good" two months, washing bugs and slugs off of tough outdoor lettuce is not very appetizing. Sometimes I'll give up a third of my indoor lettuce growing space to pak choi or another brassica, or mix in some herbs with my lettuce. And then I return to lettuce. A friend has a special growing rig dedicated to producing Swiss chard every winter. We'd both love huge crops of spinach – but lettuce and chard give bigger yields, so that's what we grow. Another more dedicated cook might find basil the must-have steady supply, or mint for mojitos and tea.

These crops have a lot in common. As introduced in Chapter 2, we harvest the leafy vegetative growth, not the fruits or seeds. So there are only two growth stages of interest – germination (seed to seedling), followed by vegetative growth. We dissuade these plants from entering reproductive maturity as long as possible, and harvest their leaves along the way. When we can't stave off maturity any longer, we take a final harvest and start over.

Some greens are more heat-tolerant than others, and some herbs prefer warmth. But cool temperatures are the ideal for most greens, between 60° -70° F [16 to 21 C], with 80° F the upper limit [26 C]. This is a comfortable match to human indoor temperatures. Be careful of heat from grow-lights or sun. The brightly lit spot will be warmer than the rest of the house. For the rest of this chapter, I refer to this temperature regime as "standard for leafy greens."

Greens have modest light needs, compared to the fruiting plants. A bright windowsill may be fine. Given a choice between east, south, or west-facing windows, pick east, for a cooler micro-climate. Or, the DIY seedling shelf presented in Chapter 5 is perfect for growing your own greens and herbs. Or you can grow greens around the lower-light periphery of a brighter light. But intense lights and sunny windowsill spots are often too warm. You could even grow greens under a basic desk lamp with a 14 W to 23 W 6500K CFL. If using artificial lights, time them 12 to 16 hours a day. This is also "standard for leafy greens."

Greens have modest nutrient needs, too. For most, the maximum hydroponic feed is 80% of the "growth stage" formula for your nutrients. If growing in soil instead, use a very light hand with the fertilizer. I'll refer to this regime as "standard for leafy greens" as well.

There are also differences between the crop families within the leafy greens camp. In the rest of this chapter, we focus on the special considerations of each type of crop. The chapter closes with some DIY projects.

Lettuce

Recommended Varieties: Summer crisp, Korean lettuce, romaines, salad bowl and other heat-tolerant loose-leaf lettuces, bibb. "Summer crisp" varieties last a long time, stand up to winter dry heat, or summer heat, and have good flavor with a bit of crunch. Loose-leaf and bibb grow fastest, but may go limp in winter dryness. Romaines grow much like summer crisp, though not all are heat-tolerant. Korean lettuce is unusually long-lived and heat-tolerant with strong pliant leaves used as a food wrap, as with spring rolls. Mesclun mixes typically include brassicas mixed with lettuce.

Varieties to Avoid: Iceberg and other firm heading types.

Soil vs. Hydroponic: Grows up to twice as fast hydroponically. Easy to grow, either way.

Time: Hydroponically, can begin harvesting a few leaves in 3 weeks from seed for loose-leaf lettuce, 4 weeks for summer crisp and romaines – half the time to maturity listed on the seed packet. Useful lifespan depends on temperature and variety – usually 8 to 10 weeks in hydroponics.

Soil: Small shallow root system, 4" depth is enough. Adult lettuce needs 6" spacing, but can grow at 3" spacing and harvest most of the plants small. A windowbox on a windowsill would work. Never over-fertilize lettuce. Many potting mixes already have enough fertilizer.

Hydroponic Nutrients: Mild, standard for leafy greens. Use seedling strength nutes until seedlings have a couple true leaves larger than the seed leaves – at least 1 week for faster varieties, 2 weeks for romaines. Then switch over to no higher than 80% of the aggressive growth recipe for your nutrients. EC 0.6 first week or two, 1.6 thereafter, if you have an EC meter.

Water: Highly sensitive to water quality. Thrives in rain water. Wants 6.0 to 7.0 pH. Winter heated air, or air-conditioning, can dry out lettuce leaves. Misting with a spray bottle can help if the lettuce looks limp instead of crisp.

Light: Standard for leafy greens.

Temperature: Standard for leafy greens. Frost kills most lettuce.

Starting: Easy. Germinate in 1 to 3 days hydroponically, or as per seed packet in soil. Seeds require light to germinate – cover the seeds barely if at all. Some lettuce variety seeds rot instead of sprouting if they're too wet. In soil, lettuce can take a month or more to reach any significant size, so it's good to start replacement plants in compact 6-packs alongside larger plants, to keep production up.

Harvesting: Cut outer leaves from plants with scissors, no more than half the leaves at a time. Alternatively, with romaines, you can cut the whole head off about an inch above the base, and it will regrow once or twice. Lettuce loses nutrients quickly after harvest, and thin-leafed varieties go limp in dry air. Best to harvest right before eating.

End-Game: Lettuce bolts when it reaches reproductive maturity – starts stretching a long stem between leaves. You can postpone this with cool temperatures, but once bolting begins, you can't stop or reverse it. Just harvest the plant and start over.

Comments

Browned, burned edges on lettuce, and yellowing older leaves, are usually a sign of too much fertilizer, pH too acidic or basic, or other water quality issue. Bottom leaves also yellow if they don't get enough light.

Freckles on lettuce leaves indicate a red lettuce variety – it's not an illness. When the lettuce is bigger, how red the leaves get depends on the variety, light, and temperature. Generally, lower temperatures and bright light favor redness. Silvia red romaine and Korean red lettuce get the deepest red of the varieties I've tried.

Aphids are fond of lettuce, and awfully hard to clean out of live plants. I put a little dish detergent in a bowl of cold water, and harvest straight from the plants into the sudsy water. Dead aphids fall off the leaves and sink to the bottom of the bowl. Then rinse, and dry with a salad spinner. The same detergent water will kill aphids on standing plants. But living plants are hard to wash, aphids are born pregnant, and you won't get all of them. They won't stay gone for long. To protect my other plants, I often just harvest out short-lived plants like lettuce that become aphid-infested indoors.

Lettuce seeds are only viable for a year or so, so don't stock up.

If you ever have too much lettuce all at once, cream of lettuce soup is delicious and easy to make. Though lettuce is best harvested minutes before eating it, for maximum vitamin content, crispness and flavor, sometimes you need to harvest more than enough for tonight's salad.

Brassicas – Kale, Cabbage, Mustard, and Asian Greens

Recommended Varieties: Toy choi, baby pak choi, komatsuna (tastes like mild horseradish), tatsoi, arugula, mizuna, tendergreen mustard, most Asian greens. Small kale or kale harvested young, such as dwarf curled blue kale or lacinato (dinosaur) kale.

Varieties to Avoid: Cauliflower, broccoli, and broccoli raab are brassicas, but they aren't leafy greens. We harvest the buds, not the leaves. Grow those as immature fruit – next chapter – if you want to grow them indoors. I haven't grown them, because they don't seem like they'd be space-efficient. Full-size cabbages, kale, and mustards can be big plants.

Soil vs. Hydroponic: Either. Hydroponic is faster at growing kale, but I haven't seen much advantage on toy choi, cabbage, komatsuna, or tendergreen mustard.

Time: As per the seed packet. Toy choi and tendergreen mustard can harvest as fast as 4 weeks – in soil or hydroponics.

Soil: 4" to 6" depth is enough, depending on the mature size of the plant, with 2" to 8" spacing. Can grow at half spacing, then harvest some small, or mix faster and slower-growing varieties, and crop the faster ones to give the slower ones more room. A windowbox on a windowsill would work. Don't over-fertilize.

Hydroponic Nutrients: Mild, standard for leafy greens. Use seedling strength nutes, until seedlings have a couple true leaves larger than the seed leaves – at least 1 week for faster varieties, 2 weeks for slower ones. Then gradually switch over to 80% of the aggressive growth recipe for your nutrients, or less. Mild is best. EC 0.6 first week, 1.6 thereafter, if you have an EC meter.

Water: Highly sensitive to water quality, even more so than lettuce. Thrives in rain water. Wants 6.0 to 7.0 pH.

Light: Standard for leafy greens.

Temperature: Standard for leafy greens. Light frost before harvest improves the flavor of several brassicas, especially kale.

Starting: Easy. Germinate in 1 to 3 days.

Harvesting: Cut outer leaves from plants with scissors, no more than one third the leaves at a time. With pak choi and mustard greens, just grow to full size and harvest whole. To eat the larger kales and mustards raw, you may need to harvest them young, or put them through a blender. Larger leaves are too tough for salad use.

End-Game: Brassicas form buds like miniature bits of broccoli when they start to mature. You can postpone this with cool temperatures, but once maturity begins, you can't stop or reverse it. Just harvest the plant and start over.

Toy choi is a cute, tasty, fast-growing brassica. Eat raw or briefly stir-fried.

Comments

Browned, burned edges and yellowing older leaves are usually a complaint about too much fertilizer, pH too acidic or basic, or other water quality. Or too little light.

Asian seed vendors carry a broad variety of brassica hybrids, to widen your leafy horizons beyond lettuce. Brassicas can be stir-fried as well as eaten raw.

Because they have much stronger flavors than lettuce, favorite brassicas vary strongly between people. I personally hate arugula, but love the horseradish tang of komatsuna. Alas, komatsuna isn't very productive. The brassicas I grow most often are toy choi and tendergreen mustard, for their quick yields and flavor.

The quicker brassicas can grow as fast as the slower lettuces. But then you harvest the whole plant and start over, instead of having a lettuce plant to pick leaves from every few days for another month or so. Generally, for the same growing space, brassicas yield less than hydroponic lettuce.

Indoor Salad

Toy choi makes a good children's growing project, provided the child is open to eating stir-fry or raw veggies. Toy choi seeds are big enough for small fingers to handle. With only a 28-day lifespan, there's something to see as the plant grows. The mature plant shape is adorable, and the flavor is mild. You can grow a few seeds wrapped in a wet napkin alongside the real grow, so the child can see what's happening under the dirt or inside the hydroponic sponge, during the first part of the wait.

For a child with low veggie tolerance, try adding onion and a bit of sugar to a stir fry, with soy sauce and ginger or sesame seed oil, or simply a slosh of store-bought teriyaki sauce. Or, eat toy choi with the ever-popular ranch dressing or hummus as a dip – toy choi are good raw. It's fun to grow a vegetable you can't often find in supermarkets.

Spinach

Recommended Varieties: Bloomsdale long-standing (heirloom). Baby leaf. Heat-tolerant varieties are best.

Soil vs. Hydroponic: Hydrophobic – won't grow in simple deep water hydroponics.

Time: Rarely as fast as the seed packet advertises.

Soil: 6" depth, with 4" minimum spacing. Spinach needs high pH soil compared to most crops – prefers a pH of 7.0. With standard potting mixes, add maybe a teaspoon of pulverized limestone or dolomite to the soil per plant and mix thoroughly, to bring the pH up. Likes fertilizer more than lettuce and brassicas – use normal instead of mild fertilizer.

Water: Not too sensitive to water quality, but over-watering slows growth.

Light: Needs brighter light than standard for leafy greens, similar to immature fruit. If growing on a windowsill, would appreciate 6 hours of direct sun per day. Can grow in a T8 seedling shelf, but would do better with 4-tube instead of 2-tube T8 fixture.

Temperature: Standard for leafy greens.

Starting: Germinates in 4 to 7 days. Soak seeds in lukewarm water for several hours before planting.

Harvesting: Cut outer leaves from plants with scissors.

End-Game: Spinach forms buds, and then flowers. You can postpone this with cool temperatures, and try to pick off the buds, but once maturity begins, you can't stop or reverse it. Just harvest the plant and start over.

Comments

I love spinach. Alas the yields, both indoors and out, are unrewarding.

Delicious as spinach is raw, we can't digest it to utilize its full nutrients unless it's cooked. And a full bag of spinach cooks down to about two servings. Try chard or Asian brassicas for a more rewarding yield.

Swiss Chard

Recommended Varieties: Any, but Bright Lights is particularly pretty – vivid golden, magenta, crimson, white, and orange stalks, all with dark green leaf tissue. This leafy green makes a nice ornamental.

Soil vs. Hydroponic: Borderline hydrophobic – will survive but not thrive in simple deep water hydroponics. A drip system might work, but needs higher pH than the other hydrophilic crops. Easy to grow in potting mix.

Time: Takes 4 to 5 weeks to first harvestable leaves. Unlike the other leafy greens, chard does not bolt. Once established, you can harvest chard for months.

Soil: 6" depth, with 4" minimum spacing. If you give it more depth and spacing (up to 6"), you can grow bigger chard plants. But that would give bigger chard leaves, and the bigger they are, the tougher they are. Chard prefers a higher-than-normal pH – 6.5 to 7.0, but happy enough with any pH between 6.0 – 7.5. With standard potting mixes, add maybe a teaspoon of lime (pulverized limestone) to the soil per plant and mix thoroughly, to bring the pH up. Likes fertilizer more than lettuce and brassicas – normal instead of mild fertilizer.

Water: Not sensitive to water quality or quantity. Don't let it dry out too much or the leaves get tougher.

Light: Needs brighter light than standard for leafy greens. Similar to immature fruit. If growing on a windowsill, would appreciate 6 hours of direct sun per day. Can grow in a T8 seedling shelf, but would do better with 4-tube instead of 2-tube T8 fixture.

Temperature: Chard likes room temperatures. If it gets too warm (above 80° F or 26 C), the leaves grow even tougher. It doesn't mind light frost. Unusually tolerant about temperature.

Starting: Germinates in 5 to 10 days at room temperature. Soak seeds in lukewarm water for several hours before planting. The large chard "seed" is actually a small dried fruit – you get several seedlings per "seed". But you'd damage the roots if you tried to separate them. With mixed-color chard, the stem color is already visible in the seedlings.

Harvesting: Cut outer leaves with the leaf-stem from the plant stalk with scissors, at the leaf-stem base, up to one third of the foliage at a time. Chard can grow huge, but don't let any leaves get bigger than 9". Small chard leaves are tough but edible in salads, and vividly colored. Bigger chard, and the thick leaf stems, should be cooked.

End-Game: Chard seems immortal. Something will go wrong eventually, or you'll simply eat your fill of chard and want to use the space for something else. Outdoors, chard survives summer heat, frosts, even survives a mild winter if mulched. Presumably it flowers, because chard seed exists. But I haven't seen a chard go to flower.

Comments

Most people prefer the flavor and texture of lettuce, brassicas, and spinach. Chard leaves and stems are tough – the stems particularly need to be cooked.

But chard is nutrient-packed and yields well and seemingly forever. It doesn't yield as much as fast as the quicker types of lettuce. But lettuce can spend half its lifespan getting up to harvestable size, and rarely lasts more than a few months. Once chard is established, production doesn't seem to stop until you terminate it. And it's very undemanding to grow.

Swiss chard plantation in 70 liter tub under shoplight. *Photo courtesy of Beth Grem.*

The chard I've found for sale in supermarkets is way too large. You can try it – cooked – to see whether you like the flavor. But smaller leaves are more tender. The leaves and stalks are never as tender as those of adult spinach.

Radish

Recommended Varieties: Small and fast – go for radishes with a maturity time of 35 days or less. Most are listed as about 28 days on the seed packet. I prefer the mild French Breakfast type radish, others may prefer the hotter round radishes. The big radishes, like daikon and horseradish, are long-lived and not as suited to indoor growing.

Soil vs. Hydroponic: Soil.

Time: 28 to 35 days.

Soil: 4 inch depth, with 2 to 3 inch spacing. The potting mix may already have enough fertilizer, and too much nitrogen prevents the roots from plumping up.

Water: Not fussy. Moist, not soggy, for best flavor.

Light: A bit more light than standard for greens. The roots won't plump up if they get too little light. The simple two-T8 seedling shelf works well.

Temperature: Standard for leafy greens. Temperatures above 80° F [26 C] will prevent the plant from forming a plumped radish root.

Starting: Germinates in 3 to 6 days. Soak seeds in lukewarm water for several hours before planting.

Harvesting: Pull up complete plant when time is up, subtracting time to germinate. (A 28 day radish that took 4 days to sprout, should harvest by about day 32 when grown indoors.) The green leafy tops are edible. My guinea pigs enjoy the greens more than I do.

End-Game: When mature, you should see a little widened dome of the top of the radish at the base of the plant. If you wait too long to harvest, the radish can get tougher or hotter, or the flavor can go off. If the radish isn't forming a plump root, and you've waited the time listed on the seed pack plus a week or two, it isn't going to happen.

Comments

Radishes aren't a particularly generous yield, except that people are satisfied with eating one or two as a garnish, or grated into a salad dressing. Because of that, you can easily grow all the radishes you want in a small plastic tub on a windowsill.

Radishes are easy to grow, and quick. They would make an ideal children's growing project, except that they're a bit strong for the average child's palate.

French breakfast radishes plumping at age 24 days, in pink tub on a seedling shelf.

Carrots, on the other hand, are delicious to children. On first glance, the carrot seems very similar to the radish, right? Not so – radishes are a brassica. The leafy greens relatives of the carrot include parsley, dill, and fennel, not radish. We eat the storage root of the small radishes when they are immature and highly perishable, because mature radishes taste bad. Carrot roots take over two months to develop, with good sun and fairly deep soil. That's too much time, space, and light to make a good indoor spectator sport for kids. Though it can be done, if you're determined and have a lot of light.

The much larger horseradish and daikon radish are eaten large and mature, like carrots – and like carrots, they're less suited to indoor growing.

Herbs

It's hard to generalize about growing herbs, because there are so many herbs, from such different plant families.

Most popular kitchen herbs come from just three genera – Labiatae, Umbelliferae, and Allium. Labiates include basil, sage, rosemary, thyme, mints, oregano, savory, sage, lavender, catnip, and lemon balm. The umbel name refers to the queen-anne's-lace style of flat radial flower. The carrot is a familiar umbel, as are parsley, dill, fennel, anise, chervil, cumin, and coriander (cilantro). The umbels tend to concentrate flavor in their seeds, as well as their leaves. Allium is the onions, including chives and garlic. Other popular herbs are scattered through many genera – ginger, bay laurel, capers, hibiscus, and the list goes on.

It's surprising to me how few plant genera we've developed for the lion's share of our food supply, yet how many plants have flavoring and medicinal uses.

On to growing some for home use.

Unusually tidy Aerogarden herbs (posted by Jewleeia on Aerogardenmastery.com).
Back row: basil, chives, thyme, purple basil. Front row: savory, mint, oregano.

Basil

The easiest herb to grow in the home. Basil grows much like lettuce, including the huge advantage in growing hydroponically – start harvesting leaves in only 3 weeks. Basil varieties abound, including a lemon basil that makes a nice herb tea, licorice-flavored Thai basil, and the familiar pesto basil. And yes, it is realistic to grow enough fresh basil indoors to make pesto. Though often people choose variety over quantity when selecting kitchen herbs to grow.

Because basil grows so quickly, I sometimes mix a pod or two of basil into a hydroponic lettuce grow. Basil is the only herb this works well with. Other herbs take longer to grow to useful size, so their lifespans don't synchronize well with lettuce. While basil also outlasts lettuce, replacement basil grows so quickly that it's no tragedy to terminate a basil plant when replanting the lettuce.

Be sure to start pinching the growth tops off basil when they have 6 true leaves or so. Pinching growth tips – and especially pinching off a top that's trying to form flowers – makes your basil grow bushier and last longer. With leafy herbs, leaf production and flavor suffers if you let them flower, and they put energy into completing their life cycle instead of continuing to churn out tasty leaves. So, harvesting basil is a balance between picking leaves to use, and pinching off tops. Smaller leaves – including from the pinching – tend to have the most flavor.

If growing basil with other herbs, harvest the fast-growing basil frequently to prevent it from crowding out and stunting your slower-growing herbs.

Basil is extra cold-sensitive, and gets sunburnt if introduced to full sunlight too abruptly. Be careful and gradual about moving a pot of basil outdoors. I grow extra basil outdoors in the summer months to complement my summer tomato harvests. If growing on a windowsill, basil would appreciate the warmer south-facing and west-facing windows.

√ **Tip:** Pinch basil, oregano, thyme, mint, sage, and rosemary.

Parsley, Dill, Oregano, and Thyme

All handy herbs to have around for cooking, these grow well together hydroponically from seed. I'd recommend including some basil with them in a hydroponic herb grow, especially since the basil is harvestable long before the rest. They all grow fine in potting mix, but more slowly. Buying plants from a nursery is quicker, but not necessary. You're growing these as annuals, so buying seed can save you money on replanting over a few years, if you find you're really using the herb.

When growing in soil, I'd keep these herbs in separate pots, to keep their quantities tuned to how much of them I want rather than how aggressively they grow. The more aggressive herbs can crowd out a weaker but useful herb.

Most of these herbs are tender annuals. (Oregano is perennial and survives a New England winter.) You can put them outside for the free sunlight in summer, but be careful about cold nights. With annuals, that's most likely a one-way trip – put them outdoors in summer, but grow a new collection for indoors in the fall.

Rosemary, Mints, Sage, and Chives

These do not grow well hydroponically, nor from seed, though for different reasons. I'd buy them as small plants and keep each in a separate pot, not artistically mixed in with others. Rosemary and sage are perennials – they take a long time to get started, and can live for years. The mints often don't breed true from seed, so starting them from seed doesn't work well for specialty mints. If you want apple mint or chocolate mint, or specifically peppermint or spearmint, go to a plant nursery and rub the leaves to test the scent. Mints propagate by spreading roots, so it's particularly important to give them a pot to themselves. They'll invade whatever root space is available.

Chives can be grown from seed, and individual chive plants are annual. But they grow in attractive self-propagating clumps, with pretty purple puffball flowers. I bought a little pot of chives once – over 15 years ago. Now they grace four planters in a different house. They'd grace a lot more if I didn't keep weeding them out. I don't eat them very much, but they're pretty in the spring and fall.

These herbs would do better on a sunny windowsill than in the weak light of a two-T8 seedling shelf.

Except for the chives, keep these herbs pinched for bushy growth. If you have outdoor space, they'll happily move indoors and out with the seasons. Just be sure to harden indoor plants gradually when moving them out into full sunlight for the warmer months. Take them out for only a couple hours at a time at first, in a sheltered location, and work up to the full challenge of the outdoor location you intend for them.

Coriander / Cilantro

Cilantro is the Spanish name for coriander. It's familiar from its use in Mexican cooking, where it adds a fresh flavor to dishes like guacamole and salsa, much like fresh parsley. You can grow cilantro in deep water hydroponics, though it's hydrophobic getting started – the seed won't germinate if it's too wet. But cilantro is a big plant once it gets going. I'd recommend growing it from seed in a pot on a windowsill, and moving it outdoors in summer to really take off, to complement summer tomatoes and peppers.

Green Onions

OK, green onions are more vegetable than herb. But it's a handy addition to a sunny herb windowsill. Cut off the green tops from some green onions you buy at a market, then plant the white bases in potting mix, to generate new green tops.

Other Herbs

The list above included all the herbs I've personally grown successfully indoors – and all the herbs I've wanted to grow indoors. But people's taste in herbs varies wildly. It just depends on what you want them for. Pesto? Mojitos? Cat treats? Salsa? Herb tea? Health tonic?

The Aerogrow company offers other herb seed pods, so they must also grow successfully in deep water hydroponics, to some extent: catnip, chervil, lavender, marjoram, savory, tarragon, and lemon balm. (Note: lemon basil is much stronger than lemon balm for herb tea, in my experience.) Unsurprisingly, Aerogrow offers eight varieties of basil – basil really thrives in an Aerogarden, and fresh basil is awfully handy to have around for cooking. Anything that can succeed in an Aerogarden can also succeed as an indoor potted plant – or possibly grow even better as a potted plant. Aerogrow also offers chives, three types of mint, cilantro, and sage pods, though I'd recommend sticking to soil for those. They grow weakly in an Aerogarden, and take a long time to reach harvestable size.

Project: Hydroponic Lettuce

In truth, my best beginner recommendation for growing lettuce indoors is the Aerogarden line of hydroponic devices from Aerogrow. These devices are often on sale, and for $80 you can get a small 3-pod Aerogarden complete with lettuce seeds, pods, nutrients, and on-board lights and timer. Within 1 to 3 days of plugging it in, your lettuce will be growing. Within 3 to 4 weeks, you'll be harvesting it. It really does seem to grow right before your eyes. The harvests will last 5 weeks or so, depending mostly on temperature. My love of indoor salad growing was born with this device, and a lot of other people feel the same way.

You could make a deep water culture hydroponic rig yourself, much like Aerogrow's but with larger capacity. Or buy such a hydroponic system for $50 on Amazon – minus the lights, seeds, and nutrients, which add up. But if you're new to hydroponics, it's easiest to start with the plug-and-play Aerogarden, to grow lettuce and the more lettuce-like herbs.

Brassicas like kale and toy choi are a different story. They grow well in hydroponics. But they grow nearly as well in potting mix. You might have more growing room for less money, and thus bigger harvests, if you use potting mix. Purely a matter of convenience and style.

That leaves two other possibilities for a DIY project for this chapter: potting mix, and *manual* hydroponics – less expensive, and no power required.

Project: Brassicas in Potting Mix

Need:

- Grow lights or moderately good natural light
- Shallow planter – windowbox shape is good – self-watering optional
- Fluffy potting mix, or potting mix + 1/3 perlite by volume
- Brassica seeds (one or two from toy choi, tendergreen mustard, mizuna, tatsoi, komatsuna)

Fill your planter with potting mix – something like Miracle Gro standard (not moisture control or organic) or some high-quality fluffy potting mix. If you wish to use an organic potting mix, buy perlite as well, and cut the potting mix with 1/3 perlite.

Keep the potting mix as fluffy as you can – don't compact it. Dampen the soil before planting seeds. For a self-watering pot, you add potting mix to the pot in layers – put some in, and water it thoroughly to establish wicking between soil and reservoir. Add mix, water, mix, water, until the container is fully nearly to the brim with potting mix.

This soil is shallow, so a self-watering planter with a bottom water reservoir is optional. You could use any windowbox with drainage.

Plant seeds at the depth listed on the package, at about 1 inch spacing [2.5 cm]. Place the pot in light right away. A bright window that gets only a couple hours of direct sun a day – but light all day – is good. A light fixture like the seedling shelf would be better, because you need to keep the plants cool.

Never let the plants dry out. The self-watering planter helps with that. If indoor air is very dry and the greens look droopy, use a spray bottle to mist the leaves.

You should see seedlings in just a few days. Let them all grow until they start to touch. Then gradually harvest whole plants – and eat them – until the remaining plants are 6 inches apart.

By age 5 weeks or so, you can harvest the bigger, outer leaves every few days, taking no more than 1/3 of the plant mass at a time. Harvest strategically to reduce crowding. Toy choi are harvested whole.

To keep a perpetual harvest going, you can start growing replacement seedlings when your greens are about 2 months old. Use a small container next to the self-watering planter for this. Then the baby replacements can get good light without competition.

Eventually, after several generations, the fertilizer in the potting mix will wear out – about when it says so on the potting mix bag. You can buy the same sort of potting mix granules to replenish the potting mix, rather than replacing it. I've used Dynamite and Osmocote brands with good results.

Variations

You can grow also grow lettuce this way. They just take longer. Or, mix fast and slow lettuce varieties. With romaines, you can optionally use cut-and-come-again as a harvest method. Using a scissors, cut the whole head of lettuce off an inch above the base, and let the whole plant grow back. Alternating plants between leaf-harvesting and cut-and-come-again, helps relieve crowding.

Brassicas grow the same way as lettuce in potting mix. I'm especially fond of the 28-day harvests of toy choi and tendergreen mustard, and the horseradish flavor of the slower komatsuna. Radishes are also easy and take 28 days. With many of these, especially the fast ones, you grow them to harvest size, then harvest the whole plant and start over.

You can grow other greens this way, but be aware of incompatibilities. For example, kale wants to grow much larger than the recommended varieties. Spinach and chard want less acidic soil.

Project: Lettuce Splasher – Manual Hydroponics

You can grow hydroponic lettuce and other greens without electricity. This is another great kid's project, if your child likes lettuce or toy choi. No air pump or bubbler system is necessary. You provide the nutrient aeration by draining and splashing by hand, twice a day.

I saw this system first from a friend called Drann online. Being an environmentally conscientious type, I just had to try it. It's a fun and cheap introduction to hydroponic growing.

Buying parts to make the splasher is problematic, in that the components are sold in bulk quantities – too much for the task at hand. More on that topic in the variations.

Four week old summercrisp lettuce growing in splashers.

- A grow light or moderately good natural light – great for windowsills
- Two 1-quart plastic freezer storage containers [1 liter]
- Two grow sponges
- One-part hydroponic nutrients, for vegetative growth (not fruiting)
- Hydroton grow rocks, or growstones, or perlite
- Seeds – summer crisp lettuce or toy choi recommended
- Transparent plastic wrap

Place grow sponges in a bowl of lukewarm water to soak for at least 15 minutes.

Take one of the plastic containers, and drill or melt four holes in the middle of the bottom for quick drainage. I use the tip of a soldering iron to melt drainage holes, but there are many ways to make holes in plastic, including a power drill, or hammering a nail through. You want big enough holes that when you fill the container with water, it completely drains in 10 seconds or so.

Wash your rocks, to rinse off any dust. Do this outdoors if possible – floating rocks and rock dust aren't good for in-sink garbage disposals or pipes.

Half-fill your holed container with grow rocks. Then take the wet sponges and lodge them into the rocks, as far apart as possible. Fill around the sponges with wet rocks. You want the tops of the sponges just barely above the rocks, and a half inch [1.5 cm] below the top of the container.

At this point, the rocks and sponges must be *wet*. Pour water through again to make sure of that point, but then discard the water. Soggy sponges can prevent germination, so the tubs are only wet, not full of liquid, until the seeds sprout.

Nest the holed container into the whole container.

Plant lettuce seeds by nestling them in the tops of the grow sponges, so they get moisture from the sponges, but get enough light to germinate. All seeds should be visible. Four seeds per sponge is enough.

Wrap the top of the tubs with plastic wrap, to keep it humid inside, and place in the growing light. Ideally, fold some opaque paper or something around the sides of the tub to prevent algae growth. Check once a day for germination. Add a dribble of water to the sponges if they seem less moist. With lettuce or brassicas, you can expect the seeds to sprout in three days or less.

Once the seeds sprout, mix a 2-liter bottle of nutrient solution using your one-part hydroponic nutrients and water. Mix this at the *mild* growing formula for your nutrients. For instance, if the instructions say to use 1 to 2 teaspoons per gallon of water, that means 1 teaspoon per gallon for mild growth, so use ½ teaspoon for your 2-liter bottle. This is the regular strength adult nutrient solution for your splashers. Mix one cup of that with one cup of water, for half-strength nutrients. Fill your tubs with the half-strength nutrients *once*. You can discard any half-strength leftovers. When filled, the water level should be about an inch [2 cm] below the top of the rocks.

Splash the splasher. Lift the holed tub to drain, splashing, into the whole tub below. Then let the holed tub sink back down into the lower tub. What you're doing here is aerating the roots and rocks and water, manually. So you want some splash. Repeat. Keep as much liquid as possible in the tubs without the lower tub overflowing. Then place the splasher back in the growing light. You don't need the plastic wrap after the seeds sprout.

One to three times a day, splash the splasher. For seedlings, keep the liquid topped up by adding plain water, because the baby roots need time to grow down into the rocks. The more often you splash, the happier the plants will be. That said, they won't die if you forget for a day.

When true leaves emerge, so you can tell the seedlings apart, thin to 1 to 2 seedlings per sponge. Thin by clipping spare seedlings out with a scissors, don't tug. A single plant per sponge will grow best, but you may want to try some of everything that comes up. The thinned seedlings are good to eat.

One week after germination, dump the weak nutrients, rinse the tubs and rocks without disturbing the plants, and refill the splasher with regular strength nutrients. From then on, dump and rinse and refill this way once a week. You'll be amazed how much the plants grow the day after a refill! Top up with plain water between refills, if the liquid gets too low to splash.

You could begin harvesting outer, lower leaves in 3 to 4 weeks. Harvest no more than 1/3 of the plant at a time, and give it a few days to recover before picking again. Remove any yellow or brown leaves.

Variations

I've used a greens splasher successfully for Korean red lettuce, summer crisp lettuce, loose-leaf lettuce, komatsuna, and kale. For light, I've used it in a seedling shelf, under a hanging CFL clamp lamp, and in the spillover light between two Aerogardens. Or you could place the splasher on a windowsill. Or put it under a CFL crookneck desk lamp to keep you company at your desk, as a constructive fidgetable.

I used to sell a kit for the splasher, because there are quantity problems in buying these parts for yourself – like a 5 year supply of nutrients, enough grow rocks for 15 splashers, enough lettuce seed and sponges for 60 of them. But the item wasn't popular enough to make the business practical.

But you can buy the parts elsewhere. Any hydroponic nutrients or grow sponges could be used, including an Aerogarden kit. Rapid Rooters is a grow sponge brand name. Park Seed, Gurneys, Burpee, and other seed companies all sell seed-starter sponges. They all work. If you have a hydroponic store nearby, they might be willing to sell you just a few grow sponges or small rockwool cubes, and just one tub worth of grow rocks. Or, to substitute for the grow rocks, you can buy small bags of perlite or vermiculite at garden centers.

Aerating a small lettuce splasher made from a 15oz ricotta tub and a coffee can.
The half gallon splasher to the right holds two varieties of kale, wrapped in a basket.

There are endless variations on the two nested tubs. You just want the inner, hole-y tub to have enough root space, and reach well down into the reservoir of the outer whole container. The outer styling and light-barrier is up to you. I prefer 3 to 4 cups capacity for the inner container, but smaller and bigger tubs work, too.

There's a limit to how big a plant is feasible to grow in a single splasher. Because of the constant care required, I'd stick to small, short-lived greens, or leafy herbs like basil. I've grown mimulus flowers as well, but most flowers aren't well-suited to the splasher. Hydrophobic crops would not be happy in this system – spinach is not an option.

I've also seen seed-starter systems that are a bigger and more sophisticated version of the Park Starts block, but still sponges in styrofoam. They suggest that works for growing greens to harvest. That might be another low-cost manual hydroponic rig, but I haven't tried it.

Summing Up

Greens and herbs – the leafy crops – are among the easiest crops to grow, and most rewarding. Harvests are large enough and useful enough that once you start, you'll want to keep these growing. As more people discover this indoor niche of urban farming, new products are coming out to make growing easier, more attractive, and suited to more homes.

Try growing some greens indoors. You may just find yourself getting addicted to indoor vegetable gardening.

Next we move on to the flowering crops. Chapter 7 covers the immature fruits, such as cucumbers, and Chapter 8 the mature fruits, peppers and tomatoes.

indoor salad

Chapter 7
Immature Fruits
Cukes, Beans, and Eggplant

It's a shame, really, that the American holy grail of salad growing is the tomato. Because cucumbers are ever so much more rewarding! Now, I know you're thinking of those dark green waxed torpedo cucumbers at the market, full of huge seeds and squash guts. (Yes, they really are dipped in wax.) And green beans? Ho-hum.

But it doesn't have to be that way. There are lots of varieties of cucumber. The waxed torpedo variety is simply productive and tough enough to survive shipping. They're not the best tasting cucumbers. A good, fresh cucumber needs no paring – the skin is delicious, too. "Burpless" varieties have small seeds, limited squash guts, delicious skins, and yes, cause less burping. Even at the supermarket, better tasting varieties are becoming available, freshly grown nearby in hydroponic greenhouses, and wrapped in plastic instead of dipped in wax.

Green beans come in varieties too – including purple and yellow beans. There, though, I have to admit, they all taste a lot alike to me. Except for asparagus ("yard-long") beans, which taste a bit like mushrooms. But whatever their flavor, they're better fresh. As in, picked just before eating. Beans are great for snacking fresh off the vine or bush.

This is completely non-obvious, but other "immature" fruits include broccoli, cauliflower, and zucchini. I haven't grown these indoors myself, because I don't love them the way I love cucumbers, and the way my kid loves green beans. But you could probably grow them indoors.

Unlike their relatives zucchini and cucumbers, melons and winter squash are not immature fruits. They're fully mature, take months of summer sun and heat, and lots of space, to eventually produce just a few fruits per plant. Not an indoor living space project at all.

Eggplant are a special case. I'm torn whether to put them in this chapter or the next. Eggplant are better if you don't let them mature. Once the plant is established, the fruit grow to harvest size faster than tomatoes and peppers. Because of that, I'd call a small eggplant, like the variety Fairy Tale, an immature fruit. This is a borderline case, though. In terms of growing tricks, as well, eggplant is intermediate between the immature and mature fruit groups.

As mentioned in Chapter 2, Plant Tech, all the salad crops go through the same life stages – sprouting, vegetative growth, flowering, and fruiting. The difference is what stage of the plant we want to eat. The previous chapter focused on leafy vegetables. Those we try to keep in vegetative growth as long as possible. We prevent them from flowering and going to seed, to keep their energy focused on producing lots of great-tasting leaves. In this chapter, instead we want to eat the immature fruits.

Immature fruits taste better immature. But also, if you let them mature, the plant completes its life cycle and stops producing. (Except for eggplant.) So keep them picked.

As the plant moves into fruiting phase, with immature fruits, it needs everything that the vegetative phase needed, plus some. The pluses are:

- More light.
- More room.
- More heat – cukes, beans, and eggplant are summer crops.
- Possibly more time.

I say "possibly" more time, because actually, you could harvest your first cukes and beans faster than a mature head of romaine lettuce grown in soil. The immature fruits aren't speed demons, but they are faster and more productive than the mature fruits. And they are generally slower and less productive than the leafy crops. They need just as much foliage and root mass – or more – to support the small part of the plant that we want to eat. So with immature fruits, you can expect lower yield per investment in space and light than you'd get with the leafy crops.

The immature fruit crops with the best indoor payoff are cucumbers, beans, and eggplant. But you need to be selective about what varieties of them to grow indoors.

Another thing the immature fruits have in common is that they're easier to grow in soil than hydroponically. This is far from obvious. Many of the best tasting cukes in the supermarket are grown hydroponically. Surf the web and you'll find gorgeous pictures of hydroponic cucumber plants, growing in simple DWC (deep water culture) hydroponic tubs. Gorgeous big green plants, with their first flowers opening. But are they actually producing mature cucumbers? You won't find many pictures of that.

Socrates and Tasty Jade cucumbers – this grow lasted a year and produced
99 cucumbers from two plants.

Cucumbers need to develop a lot of root mass to support developing fruit. If you raise them kindly, provide for all their needs, give them unlimited well-aerated water, enable them to grow rambunctiously without investing in much root mass at all, you grow stunningly beautiful, lush vegetative stage cucumber plants. Then they develop fruit, and the plants crash, small root systems unable to cope with the sudden huge water demand of developing fruit.

This isn't just with hydroponics, by the way. I've grown cucumbers outdoors in soil for 30 years. I plant the seeds in so-so soil, water only when necessary, and give them some acidic fertilizer when they look tired. Then they grow and produce like crazy. But when I tried to grow them in my GrowBoxes, with essentially unlimited water, and tomato-friendly nutrients high in calcium, they didn't last long once they tried to set fruit.

Beans have a similar story, though not the same. It's best not to give beans any nitrogen fertilizer at all. Again, they grow a hugely lush vegetative plant if grown too kindly, and not many beans. In the GrowBoxes, my pole beans grew 6 feet tall and produced no beans at all. The one time I tried to grow bush beans hydroponically, they developed a truly revolting clear ropy slime in the nutrient tank – and no beans. But, simply push bean seeds into so-so soil and give them some quality benign neglect, water only when the soil dries out and – *voilà*. Beans.

In theory, one might expect peas to grow much like beans. My attempts to grow peas indoors haven't been too successful, though. It took me about 3 years' practice to hit upon a strategy to grow them outdoors successfully. That strategy involves getting pre-sprouted peas into the ground in the half-frozen March of Connecticut, to get maximum mileage out of our short cold spring. That doesn't bode well for indoor pea growing. But if you have a cold and sunny 3-season porch, peas might be worth a try. At best, they're a fairly low-yield crop, though. It's a shame, because fresh-picked peas are delicious. There is no way to eat them fresh enough, except to grow them yourself. After picking, pea sugars rapidly turn to starch, within hours. Unlike most vegetables, the best-tasting peas you can buy are frozen.

Eggplant, again, is the marginal case. Eggplant is easy to grow in a self-watering pot, and productive with similar benign neglect, though they want more water and fertilizer. But eggplant thrive easily enough in DWC hydroponics, too, such as an Aerogarden. They use the same nutrient mix you'd give a tomato, only weaker.

And again – all of the immature fruits need light. The lights that are adequate for lettuce and other leafy plants will only be enough for the immature fruit group plants when they're small. As they grow, they need light over more area, because most are bigger plants. But they also need more intense light over that area, to bear fruit. Given a choice of sunny windows, these warmth-loving plants would benefit from southern or western exposure.

Like the leafy greens, we arrest development on the immature fruits, but at a different stage of life. With these crops, make sure they never grow a mature fruit, because then they complete their life cycle and stop producing. Eggplant are the exception. A mature eggplant fruit doesn't shut down production. It just doesn't taste very good, and the seedy texture is unpleasant. A mature eggplant fruit is one that has lost its shiny gloss, and gone to a dull matte finish.

Around the web, you'll see all sorts of advice to switch completely to red lights for fruiting. This advice is targeted for the mature fruit group, not the immature fruits. And I don't entirely agree with it for the mature fruit group, either. Immature fruit plants should never stop their vegetative growing, and need the bluer wavelengths of light for their whole lives.

Next up, some reference notes on each of these crops. A DIY cucumber project closes the chapter.

Cucumber

Recommended Varieties: Socrates, Tasty Jade, Zeina.

When selecting your own varieties, features to look for: good for greenhouse growing, tolerant of cool temperatures (for a cucumber), self-pollinating, seedless, burpless. Compact would be nice, but I haven't found that feature combined with the other, more important features.

Varieties to Avoid: Tendergreen – it just doesn't succeed indoors.

Soil vs. Hydroponic: Soil. Can grow hydroponically, but not recommended for deep water culture. A drip-based system might work.

Time: What's listed on the seed package is a minimum. I've harvested in as little as 7 weeks. The start of production is highly dependent on temperature and light. After that, I've had cucumber plants survive and produce for as long as 12 months.

Soil: Average potting mix. A 14" self-watering pot (16 quarts of soil) can support 1 or 2 cucumber plants. Needs extra drainage – add rocks or perlite to lower layer of soil. Cucumbers prefer acidic soil. Potting mix is fine, but do not add limestone, dolomite, or tomato fertilizers.

Water: After the seed sprouts, don't add water unless the reservoir is dry. When the fruit are developing, this may be daily – the fruit develop fast, and are mostly water. But the roots need to dry between watering.

Light: A lot. Your power bill will thank you for leveraging a sunny window. But I've grown cukes with "only" 125 W worth of CFLs (6 hanging spotlight lamps) distributed along the length of the vine. I loop the vine back on itself to limit the volume of bright light needed. Needs primarily 6500K light, with maybe 1/3 of the bulbs of redder 4100K light, if not using sunlight. With limited winter sunlight, I use 5 bulbs instead of 6 to supplement the sun. Looping the vines under a 6-lamp 48" T8 fluorescent light fixture also works, with the lights within a couple inches of the leaves. This much light is brutal on the eyes. Use reflectors to keep the light out of your eyes and onto the plants.

Temperature: The ideal temperature for cucumbers is about 80° F [26 C], and they really slow down below 70° F [21 C]. A southern or western sunny window helps to keep them warm.

Fertilizer: Most potting mix comes with enough fertilizer built-in until the plants take off and start to vine, at age about 4 weeks (longer if they're chilly). After that, I usually use organic fertilizer as a side-dressing at the top of the pot once a month or so. When the leaves get a bit yellow and the plant looks tired and stops flowering and producing, I apply some acid fertilizer via the reservoir, such as a formulation for orchids or azaleas. Cukes like their soil more acidic than most vegetables. I've also read the opposite on the Internet. But I add acid fertilizer, and it works.

Starting: Germinates in 3 to 6 days at growing temperatures. Won't germinate in colder temperatures. Soak seeds in lukewarm water for several hours before planting.

Harvesting: Don't let cucumber fruits get mature, or the vine will stop flowering. This is trickier than you might expect, because cukes grow from tiny to mature in a matter of days, and they can hide under giant leaves or behind the pot.

Pruning: When the vine is about the maximum length your light arrangement or supports can accommodate, clip off the growing tip at the end of the vine. Usually about 6 to 8 feet [2 to 2.5 m] of vine is enough. Side shoots develop lower on the vine after tip-pruning. If the plant seems to set too many cucumbers at the same time, pinch off half of the miniature fruit or buds to get faster fruit development.

Pollinating: It's best to grow self-pollinating cucumbers indoors. But if you grow a standard two-sexed cucumber, you can pollinate them by hand. A female cucumber flower has a little pickle shape at the base that develops into a fruit. Note – at first you get only male flowers. Female flowers develop week or so later, on the same plant. Once you have open female flowers to pollinate, pinch off a male flower and rub its center tip against the center tips of the female flowers. Or, use a soft-bristled paintbrush to pick up pollen from the male flowers and paint it onto the centers of the female flowers. Some female flowers may develop into cukes even if they're never pollinated, but most won't. It depends on the cucumber variety.

Comments

If you check out the recommended varieties Socrates and Tasty Jade, you'll be amazed by the prices – the right kind of cucumber can cost nearly $1 per seed. The problem here is that the ideal indoor cucumbers are ones that don't require pollination, and thus are nearly seedless. This makes seed production expensive.

Pollinating cucumbers is worth avoiding. Cucumbers produce separate male and female flowers. To pollinate them, you catch a ripe male flower and transfer the pollen – a service kindly provided by insects outdoors. I've grown this sort of cucumber indoors, and it works, but it is an extra effort. I got lucky in that I picked a variety that was able to set fruit with or without pollination. (It was a Korean white cucumber – they're good, and like cooler temperatures than most cukes. I couldn't find those seeds again next time I looked, though.)

Normal indoor home temperatures are on the cool side for a cucumber. Try to grow them in a warm room or warm sunny window.

Indoor potted cukes are subject to some annoying insect pests – fungus gnats, and spider mites. There are biological controls you can use to disrupt the fungus gnats, but the most effective measure is to mulch the top of the soil and let it dry out completely between watering. Fungus gnat larvae die in the dry soil.

I've found nothing that can stop an indoor spider mite infestation once it gets out of hand. The first sign of spider mites is yellow freckles on the green cucumber leaves. This means the spider mites are amassing on the underside of the leaves – try to wash the bottom of the leaf immediately to forestall the inevitable, even if you can't see them. They're very small. Another sign is fine cobwebby threads. Spritzing the cucumber leaves with water in dry hot afternoon sun will slow down the mites' reproductive rate. But the spider mites may still win in the end. I keep trying to save the plant, but it would probably be wiser to just destroy the plant, dump the potting mix, wash everything thoroughly, and start over. If you see spider mite signs, by all means you can try to save the plant, or at least get a few more fruit out of it before admitting defeat. But if you have a separate place to start a new plant, without the spider mites migrating, you might want to get a replacement cucumber plant started in the meantime.

This all sound like a lot of work. But the rewards are generous. When a cucumber plant is happy and healthy, it can crank out several fruit a week, evenly spaced for your supper enjoyment. We love them simply sliced, with a dash of salt and a splash of seasoned rice vinegar, or with a splash of caesar dressing or Japanese onion dressing for a change of pace. If your eyes get tired and puffy, reserve a couple slices and sit back with the cucumber slices on your eyes for a few minutes for an anti-puffiness treatment – cucumbers are a gentle astringent. Or try a slice of cucumber in ice water for a refreshing drink.

I love cucumbers.

Beans

Recommended Varieties: Any bush bean.

Varieties to Avoid: Pole beans, unless you have a very tall window. Some pole beans – such as runner beans – are also not self-pollinating. Avoid those.

Soil vs. Hydroponic: Soil.

Time: About as listed on package. I've harvested bush beans in as little as 6 weeks.

Soil: Average potting mix. Bush beans don't need much depth – 4" will do. It doesn't greatly matter whether it's a self-watering pot, but needs drainage. Bush beans should be spaced about 4" apart. The yield per plant is modest. A windowbox shaped planter is good. Don't fertilize beans.

Water: Careful not to over-water during germination. Bean seeds rot if the soil is soggy. Afterward, let soil dry between watering, but don't let the plants wilt.

Light: Fairly bright. I've grown happy bean plants on a western windowsill with no extra light. A two-T8 lettuce shelf probably has enough light for bush beans.

Temperature: The ideal temperature for beans is about 80° F [26 C], but they're fine down to 60° F [16 C]. They'll just produce slower. Again, a sunny window helps.

Fertilizer: Potting mix usually provides more than enough fertilizer. Avoid over-fertilizing beans. Extra nitrogen makes them produce leaves instead of beans.

Inoculant: This isn't fertilizer, but beans yield better if the seed is planted with inoculant. Legume inoculant, or "bean booster," provides symbiotic soil bacteria that form nodules on the bean roots. These root-and-bacteria nodules draw nitrogen out of the atmosphere and convert it into a plant-usable form. The right bacteria are not present in potting mix, so your yields improve if you provide them. Don't let the word "bacteria" bother you – they're beneficial, and not the slightest bit interested in humans.

Starting: Germinate in 7 to 12 days at growing temperatures – a warm spot will speed them up. Soak seeds in lukewarm water for one hour before planting.

Harvesting: Use two hands to pick, so as not to damage the plants. Don't let bean pods get big and lumpy – mature beans will stop the plant's production. Bush beans tend to produce the largest crop first, set a smaller crop two weeks later, and might go a third round. Then they're done.

Pruning: Don't. Not even on pole beans – let them flop down instead.

Pollinating: Not needed for bush beans. Avoid pole beans that require it.

6 week Contender bush beans, nearing harvest, in very small pots.

Comments

Bush beans on the windowsill are a satisfying project for even the smallest children – they like eating raw green beans. And there's very little effort involved.

A bush bean yield tends to be pretty small. Outdoors, I usually grow pole beans instead. They take a couple extra weeks to get started, and then produce generously for months. But a pole bean is a huge plant – 8 feet tall [2.5 m], though not very wide. You might be able to train them to grow horizontally. But they want to grow up, with full summer heat and sunlight. If you have a tall sunny window, it might be worth a try. Pole beans are beautiful plants, and yield well. But I eat my fill in the summer, and grow bush beans now and then on a windowsill for my kid's enjoyment. I'm not fond enough of beans to pay for the amount of power it would take to light them artificially. But it could work, and I've read that other people do grow them indoors.

Legumes – the bean family – are key in natural agriculture, because they fertilize the soil instead of wearing it out. Grains are especially notable for exhausting soil. If you grew grains two years in a row in the same soil, the second year yields would be pitiful. So the millenia-old technology is to grow grains one year, and leave the field fallow the next. During fallow years, the field grows legumes like clover, peas, lentils, soybeans, or alfalfa to replenish the soil. This

117

high-protein cover crop makes great feed for the livestock. The ancient Mesopotamians had already figured this out. Variations abound. The British used a four-crop rotation system in the 18th century – wheat, turnips, barley, and clover.

That said, the green bean isn't as good at fixing nitrogen in the soil as some of its cousins, like soybeans. But you get the idea. With beans, use inoculant to help them fertilize their own soil, instead of adding nitrogen fertilizer.

Eggplant

Recommended Varieties: Fairy Tale, a bright purple-striped small eggplant.

Varieties to Avoid: Twinkle – it's a larger plant than advertised. Bambino is compact enough, but the marble-sized fruit aren't very good eating.

Soil vs. Hydroponic: Soil is easiest. Hydroponic works fine, too.

Time: 10 to 12 weeks. "Time to harvest" on an eggplant seed packet counts from transplant of plants that are already 6 weeks from seed. I don't know how long an eggplant could keep producing. At least several months.

Soil: Average potting mix. Fairy Tale is a small plant. I've grown one in a hanging-planter sized self-watering pot, holding perhaps 5 quarts of soil. Fair warning: a normal eggplant, even one advertised as "good for container growing," is not small. A full-sized eggplant is a good match size-wise for a full-sized tomato, and could happily take 5 gallons of soil – 20 quarts or liters. A few tablespoons of limestone or dolomite mixed into the soil helps, if you have it. Peppers prefer soil more basic (as opposed to acidic), and enjoy extra calcium.

Water: Eggplant like water, but they're tough. Keep the reservoir topped up, but they're OK if they go dry now and then.

Light: Bright. During the vegetative, pre-flowering stages, you can get away with low light as for greens. But by the time buds start to form, they need full-strength light and plenty of it. Fortunately, the Fairy Tale plant is small, so a sunny window will work. Using only artificial lights, try one 23 W 6500K CFL for the early growth, and add a second 23 W 4100K CFL when buds start to form. Add a third 23W CFL of either color when the plant gets bigger, for larger yields.

Temperature: Summer crop. The ideal temperature is about 80° F [26 C], but they're fine down to 60° F [16 C]. A sunny window helps.

Nutrients: Growing hydroponically, use the same system as your nutrients recommend for tomatoes – only mixed weaker than for tomatoes. Goes through four stages – very weak for germination and the first two weeks after that, then gradually switch to vegetative growth stage nutrient mix, then transition, then flowering and fruiting stage nutrients for the remainder of the plant's life. Eggplant are sensitive to the nutrients getting too acidic. Top up the reservoir with plain water between feedings, as the eggplant itself makes its nutrients more acidic. If you have an EC meter, try EC 0.6 for 4 weeks, EC 1.6 thereafter, with a pH around 6.5.

Fertilizer: Use a side-dressing of organic fertilizer at the top of the pot. (Make a long indentation in the soil, press the fertilizer's recommended dose into the groove, and water it in thoroughly.)

Starting: Germinate in 14 days at room temperature – a warm spot will speed them up. Soak seeds in lukewarm water for a few hours before planting.

Harvesting: Cut off with scissors. Don't let eggplant get too big and lose their bright shiny finish. When the shiny skin dulls, the fruit is overripe. Unlike cukes and beans, this won't shut down the plant. It just makes for an inferior harvest, with big tough seeds and poor flavor.

Pruning: Don't.

Pollinating: There's no such thing as a self-pollinating eggplant – you need to help. Fortunately it's easy. When the flowers open, gently rub the nose of each flower with finger or soft-bristled paintbrush. Eggplant don't have separate male and female flowers.

A 13-week Fairy Tale eggplant, growing in an Aerogarden.

Comments

Eggplant makes an interesting ornamental. They put weeks of effort into each big ornate origami-folded blue-violet flower, with a brilliant yellow-gold center. The glossy fruit – especially the white-streaked vivid purple of a Fairy Tale – are gorgeous. Alas, the foliage is more of a grey-green fuzzy hump, with thorns. Unlike its close relatives, the pepper and tomato, once you can see an eggplant fruit, it's not long before you can eat it. The fruit grows from nubbin to harvest in a couple weeks. They're good to eat as baby vegetables, as well as when they're bigger.

Eggplant are easy to grow, if a bit slow. But a single plant can produce more eggplant than you want to eat. A small indoor variety is really for the best. I've harvested 60 fruit from a single Fairy Tale eggplant. At 2 to 3 slender fruits per serving, that's quite a yield. And they produce continuously, providing a steady harvest stream. So although eggplant isn't really a salad vegetable, it's worth including here as perhaps the only fruiting crop that easily produces more than enough indoors, from a single plant.

One particularly memorable summer, I made the mistake of growing a Gretel eggplant outdoors in a GrowBox all to itself. That happy plant gifted me with 160 white fruit, each bigger than a Fairy Tale, over the course of about 3 months. Don't get me wrong, Gretel eggplant are delicious. But that's entirely too much eggplant. To make matters worse, I'd grown Fairy Tale indoors in the spring before the Gretel outdoors in the summer, for six straight months of eggplant overload.

Fairy Tale is a popular variety. If you start the project in the spring, you may be able to buy a young transplant, and cut 4 to 6 weeks off the wait for your first harvest.

The quickest way to cook a small eggplant is to prick it with a fork and microwave it. Or oil the skin and grill it. Alas, I don't like eggplant skin, so I normally pare, slice, and sauté them in olive oil and garlic, with a few capers. This makes a delicious pizza topping. As a side dish, it's even better if I have a tomato to sauté with the eggplant, plus some onion. This is all a great deal more effort than simply slicing a cucumber, or putting a bowl of lettuce on the table. And the range of entrees that go well with a side of eggplant is unfortunately more limited than for a side salad.

I've seen around the Internet that okra is similar to eggplant, in terms of how to grow it. I don't like okra, so I haven't tried it.

Outdoors, I found that ground cherries are also similar to eggplant – a borderline immature crop from the same plant family. They produce even faster than eggplant, and fall off the plant immature, to eventually ripen inside their cute

Indoor Salad

little Chinese lantern style husks, in a bowl or on the ground. Ground cherry plants are also conveniently plastic in size. Give them room and they get huge, give them a small pot and they produce while small. Unfortunately, I didn't much care for the flavor of the one ground cherry plant I grew – a bit like a not-sweet cherry tomato, but off somehow, not a fruity flavor at all. But if you like them, ground cherries would probably be similar to growing eggplant indoors.

Project: A Cucumber Run

Although this project prepares the pot, too, the real trick here is managing and lighting a rambunctious vine 8 feet long [2.5 m]. If you have a sunny window to leverage, by all means get the most of it. Sunny-window variations provided at the end.

Need for the pot:

- Cucumber seeds – Tasty Jade, Socrates, or Zeina work (~$10 with shipping)
- 14" diameter self-watering pot, capacity ~16 quarts soil (~$10)
- Fresh potting mix, from sealed bag, ordinary Miracle Gro (~$8)
- Grow rocks, perlite, or washed pebbles – about 2 cups
- Organic fertilizer – Dynamite plant food, for example
- Optional mulch (newspaper will do)

Need for the pen:

- Space, about 4' by 2.5' footprint [1.2m x 0.75m], by 3' high [1m], against a wall
- Two tri-fold presentation boards (48"x36" flat, 12"x 24" x 48" standing)
- 4.5' length of ¾" PVC pipe [1.35m, 23cm thick]
- 6 hanging lamp cords
- Heavy-duty timer (3-prong grounded outlet)
- 6-plus outlet surge protector strip
- Long twist-ties for cord management
- 6 CFL spotlights (built-in reflectors), 23 W or so, 4 x 6500K, 2 x 4100K
- (Optional) plant stands or other bit of platform furniture about pot-height

The Plants

Prepare the pot with extra rocks or perlite at the bottom. As with all self-watering pots, pack soil into the wicking section that reaches down into the reservoir, and water that in thoroughly. For the next several inches of soil, mix rocks or perlite into the potting mix, and water that layer in. Then fill the rest of the pot, watering in. These cucumber seeds are expensive, so plant only 2 or 3 seeds, for 1 or 2 plants. If this is your first time growing cucumbers, start with only 1 plant. But the pot is big enough for 2.

Cucumber seeds are planted 1 inch deep, and germinate in the dark. Soak the seeds for a few hours in lukewarm water before planting to help them germinate faster. Keep the soil moist but not soggy until the seedlings emerge.

You don't need to turn on any lights until seedlings emerge. And don't waste power giving them more light than they need – the seedlings will be happy with only 1 spotlight turned on until they're nearly a month old. Add the rest of the lights as the vines grow long enough to reach them.

The Cucumber Run

Now for the pen. The basic idea is to put the pot at one end of a 4'x2' enclosure, and let the vines ramble out to the other end, turn, and head back toward the pot. Spotlights hang along this run, pointing down at the vines. It's more convenient if you have some other bit of furniture supporting the vines at about the same height as the pot, but not required. Bits of furniture about the right shape include plant stands, a bit of half-height closet organizer, or a couple over-the-sink organizer shelves.

Ideally, the pen should be in a warm location in your home. Cucumbers grow and produce much faster when warm.

Take the tri-fold presentation boards. Cut off one 12"x36" panel from each board and reserve them. So now you have two two-folds, and two spare pieces. Arrange the two-folds around your cucumber run area. You want short 12" sides at both ends, to rest the PVC pipe on. And the 24" sides of the two-folds meet at the middle of the run on the room side. The wall forms the back side. Once you've decided which board bits are the ends for your run, cut a notch in the middle-top of those 12" sections, to rest the PVC pipe on.

Cucumber pen, overhead view. The lights are suspended from a PVC pipe frame.

Use trash bags to line the floor of your pen. Place the pot at one end, and arrange the two-fold boards. Place the PVC pipe on top. Using twist-ties to manage the cords, hang the 6 light sockets from the PVC pipe, space them, and twist-tie the plug-end cords to the pipe for loose cord management. To begin with, you only need one 6500K CFL spotlight screwed in, above the pot. Plug all the cords into the surge strip. Plug the surge strip into the timer. When seedlings emerge, plug the timer into the wall power, and set it for 14 hours a day.

Remember, 6500K lights maximize vegetative growth – leaves and vine. And 4100K lights encourage flowering and fruiting. So as the plants grow long enough to need light, you'll turn on a second 6500K spotlight for the young plants next, then alternate 4100K and 6500K lamps to the end of the run. When the vines reach the far end of the cucumber run, all 6 CFLs will be on.

You may have picked your first cucumber by then.

When the vines reach the far end, train them to turn back toward the pot. When they reach back to the pot, the vines should be 6 or 7 feet long. That's long enough. Prune the growth tips off the vines. They'll sprout side vines along their lengths for new cucumber flowers and fresh leaves.

You have two leftover 12" x 36" pieces of foam-core board, removed from the tri-fold presentation boards. You can rest one on the top of the run to keep lights out of your eyes and reflected back down onto the plants. Save the other. At the beginning, you don't need these leftover pieces. Just don't throw them away.

Plant Care

Once your seedlings emerge, do not over-water young cucumber vines. If they go limp, water them from the top of the pot – the self-watering wicking system can hiccup sometimes. But generally, fill the reservoir and let it go completely dry before refilling. Actually, this is true of adult cucumbers, as well – but they can drink that reservoir dry in a single day. Cucumber is one of our *"hydrophobic"* plants, with a love-hate thing going on with water. It has issues with soggy roots.

Add mulch to the top of the pot after the seedlings emerge. Give the stems about an inch on all sides mulch-free – don't pile mulch against the stems. The mulch suppresses algae growing on top of the soil, and may discourage fungus gnats.

Adjust the lights to keep them 2 to 6 inches above the leaves. Since the spotlights are enclosed, leaves don't burn when they touch the lights. But leaves do block the light from other leaves.

When the plants have several true-leaves, add some organic fertilizer as a side dressing at the top, and water it in. When the vines are setting first fruit, add some more fertilizer. When the plants look tired after bearing for a month or so, add more. If the plants look really tired and take a break from producing flowers, you can usually encourage them back to life by adding some acid fertilizer mixed into their water, at usual outdoor strength. Azalea and orchid food are acid formulations.

Do not use tomato fertilizer – tomatoes like base instead of acid.

See the cucumber section earlier in this chapter for further growing tips. Key point: keep those cukes harvested. Cucumber fruits are uncannily good at hiding, and have giant leaves to hide behind. If any fruit matures, the vine will shut down and produce no more. Back to square one.

This may sound like a lot of work. And it is an investment. But after setting up the pen, there's little ongoing effort. And cucumbers can harvest in as little as 7 weeks – and keep harvesting. I had a two-plant cucumber run last 12 months once, producing a couple cukes a week on average.

Variations

Instead of supporting the PVC bar on presentation board, you could make a PVC frame – uprights as well as a long bar – or suspend the lights some other way. Then just use the presentation boards for light control on the cucumber pen, not light support.

All fruiting vegetables take bright light, so your power bill will thank you for using a sunny window – if you can. If the window only provides direct sun a few hours a day in winter, that's fine – you can still cut back to four or five CFL's instead of six. The harder problem in my home is that windows get chilly in winter. And these are summer plants. I can't grow cucumbers in front of my biggest sunny window, because it's too cold for half the year.

I position the cucumber run much the same in front of a warmer window, but use a back-reflector – a flattened-out tri-fold board. Because of the window height, I use a PVC frame to hang lights from.

Cucumbers can also be trained to climb up a string to the ceiling. How to arrange supplemental lighting for them that way, I leave to your ingenuity.

It might be cheaper to buy a 4-foot 6-lamp T8 shop-light fixture, and use 2 x 4100K and 4 x 6500K fluorescent tubes in the shop light. Or the brightness equivalents with a T5 fixture, at rather more expense. But getting the shop-light to hang 12" from a surface where the cucumber vines ramble, in a reflective enclosure, in a room warm enough for cucumbers, isn't easy to arrange in my home. To do this, I might use a 4 foot long table as the base, and arrange side reflectors out of tri-fold board. The light fixture would be dangling quite a ways down from the ceiling. And the side reflectors would tend to blow over unless secured somehow.

If you pick too many cucumbers to eat immediately, or prefer your cucumbers chilled, wrap them in plastic wrap. Otherwise they soon become flexible like a pickle, instead of crunchy. This is why supermarket cucumbers are waxed.

Summing Up

The immature fruits include cucumbers, beans, and eggplant. This is the next easiest tier of vegetables to grow indoors. They need more light and more time than the leafy greens and herbs. And for the sheer volume of plant, yields are lower, since we only eat the fruits. But they take less time than the mature fruits of the following chapter.

Next up, the American gardener's top quest: the great-tasting tomato. And peppers, both sweet and hot.

Chapter 8
Mature Fruits
Tomatoes and Peppers

Ah! That holy grail of the American gardener, the delicious home-grown tomato. Even more so than cucumbers, the supermarket mass-produced article is a sad, sad imitation of the real deal. Until I grew tomatoes at home myself for the first time, I didn't think I liked fresh tomatoes. Kind of pinkish and mealy and vapid, with sour gel and bitter seeds.

A real tomato, on the other hand, picked fully ripe, is sweet and tangy, with deep flavor reminiscent of the finest tomato sauces you've ever eaten. Once you've eaten real tomatoes, you just don't want to eat supermarket-pink ones ever again. No doubt this is why supermarkets offer a growing selection of deluxe tomatoes in the past decade. It doesn't matter how cheap they offer the vapid pink ones anymore. An ever-increasing number of people know better than to buy them. Blech.

But even the rapidly expanding tomato selection in the supermarkets is nothing compared to the thousands of varieties of tomato seed available. Yes, thousands. Tomato varieties encompass an amazing array of sizes, shapes, colors, skin thickness and crack resistance, ripening pattern, growth and harvesting habits, plant sizes, leaf styles, meat to gel ratios, disease resistance packages, temperature ranges, harvest speed – and yes, flavors. You can taste the difference between tomato varieties. And they all taste better than the vapid supermarket pink tomato.

The anonymous supermarket pink tomato is picked green, without the sugars added at the end of ripening, and allowed to sort-of ripen on its long road trip to your supermarket. There's just no comparison with a truly ripe tomato, of any variety. Even home-grown tomatoes I've picked green and left to ripen in a bag taste better than the winter supermarket pink ones.

Park's better bush tomato grown in an Aerogarden with lightscreen (Chapter 5). Got rave reviews at a show&tell – people asked the variety, so they could grow it outdoors.

So the allure of home-grown tomatoes is clear – they taste good. Alas, they are not easy to grow. Most of those thousands of tomato varieties are impractical to grow indoors due to size – a happy tomato can be a big plant. The size of the fruit isn't related to the size of the plant, by the way. Cherry tomatoes often grow on the longest, gangliest vines of them all. And indoors, sadly, you're in danger of growing tomatoes that taste as vapid as the supermarket pink article.

And that would be really sad, after you've invested the three to four months it takes the plant to deliver a fruit. Yes, tomatoes take time.

Ripe peppers can take even more time. You might like them unripe, like a green bell pepper or cubanelle or jalapeño. But being green doesn't qualify them as an immature fruit for our indoor growing purposes. They still take longer than a tomato to deliver, and require mature fruit style care and feeding. Peppers come in far more varieties than you'll find at supermarket or farm markets, though fewer than the tomato. Varieties include plant shapes from dwarf to giant, fruit shapes from cherry to bells, horns to sheep-nose, sweet peppers, hot peppers, in an amazing array of jewel-bright enamel colors – vivid green, yellow, white, cream, orange, red, purple, white, and brown.

Do peppers taste better home-grown? Not especially, for the same variety. Unlike the mushy tomato, sturdy pepper fruits travel and store quite well. But the supermarkets – and local farm markets – may not carry your particular favorites. I'm partial to the super-sweet tender horn shaped peppers, more than the popular bell peppers. And here in the Northeast, it's hard to buy the Southwestern or

Caribbean or Indian hot chilis. These really do taste different than the available supermarket varieties. And none of the available peppers are grown locally, except for a scant 2 months at the end of summer. Most of the year, peppers need to travel thousands of road miles to reach my local markets. Still, if you're not a connoisseur of exotic peppers you've never seen, it may seem a mystery that anyone would bother to grow them in-home.

Except pepper plants are beautiful. Large deep green heart-shaped leaves drape the plant, to provide a perfect backdrop for small bright white star flowers. The fruits are glossy and brilliant as enamel, regardless of what jewel-tone color they're currently sporting. Edible ornamental plants just don't come any prettier than the pepper.

Peppers are also easier to grow than tomatoes, aside from that pesky business of taking so long.

Practical? Maybe not. It doesn't have to cost $64 per fruit. But growing your own indoors might not be cheaper than buying them, either. Maybe it's a bit of a macho thing – to prove your mettle as a gardener, you want to master growing tomatoes and peppers. But mainly, most people just want to eat them, as their favorite vegetables of all.

I've been a moderator on indoor gardening Internet forums for years. From what I've seen, practical just doesn't enter into it. People often get into indoor gardening exactly because they want to grow their own tomatoes and peppers indoors. All too often, they end up with tomato heartbreak. It's not as easy as they'd hoped.

Does that sound silly? Being heartbroken over a failed tomato plant? Once you've invested money and months of your time and love and attention to a project, it isn't silly to be heart-broken when it fails. These plants share your home for a long time. It's easy to get as attached to them as you would to a pet.

You can grow great-tasting tomatoes and peppers indoors, in your home, year-round, without breaking the bank, or your heart. But please know this before you start. You won't be able to grow just any variety. They take a lot of light. And they take a lot of time. These plants go through every stage of plant development – germination, vegetation, flowering, immature fruit growth, and mature fruit growth. Each stage has different needs.

As in previous chapters, next up are some reference fact sheets on tomatoes and peppers, then a DIY project to close the chapter. Quick preview: we leave "hydrophobia" behind with the mature fruits. Tomatoes and peppers are happy in soil or hydroponics, whichever is convenient for you. As for hydroponics being quicker than soil – well, perhaps a few days quicker.

Tomato

Recommended Varieties: The wish list is *"indeterminate short internode"* or *"compact indeterminate"* or *"dwarf indeterminate"* varieties (they all mean the same thing), preferably with a good disease resistance package. Park's Better Bush for mid-size beefsteak tomatoes. Jet Star low acid slicer tomatoes. Sweet Baby Girl or Husky cherry tomatoes. Aerogarden's tested tomato kits. Tiny Tim dwarf cherry is a determinate heirloom, if heirloom is important to you.

Unrecommended Varieties: Container Choice. Red Robin. Indeterminate varieties that are not compact or dwarf.

Soil vs. Hydroponic: Whichever you prefer.

Time: 13 to 14 weeks to start harvesting cherry tomatoes, 16 to 17 weeks for mid-size. The timing doesn't change much based on temperature or plant care. An indeterminate tomato can keep producing until something goes wrong – possibly a year or more, but often 6 months.

Soil: 16 quarts of ordinary potting mix (no moisture control) in a 14" self-watering pot. A full-sized tomato wants 20 quarts (5 gallons). Skimping on soil helps dwarf the plant. A few tablespoons of limestone or dolomite mixed into the soil helps, if you have it. Tomatoes prefer soil more basic (as opposed to acidic), and enjoy extra calcium.

Fertilizer: Use a fertilizer specially formulated for tomatoes, as directed on the package, for a potted tomato. Tomatoes have special dietary needs – don't use a generic fertilizer.

Water: Keep the self-watering pot reservoir topped up, except when ripening fruit. When ripening, let the reservoir run dry between watering – tomato flavor thrives on adversity. But don't leave it dry for a whole day, or the fruit will crack.

Light: Intensely bright, 14 hours a day. Tomatoes don't have a low-light phase. Use bright light from day one. Using purely artificial lights, try one 23 W 6500K CFL for a baby plant, and work up to eight 23 W CFLs arranged around a single plant as it grows, trying to get intensely bright light within 6" of the plant, on all sides. That's for a *compact* 3' [1 m] tomato. From the time the plant starts to form its first buds, half the light should be 4100K, half 6500K. If using a sunny window, augment with artificial lights in winter. Fluorescent T8 lights aren't intense enough for tomatoes, though T5HO or HID or LED lights would work. Tomatoes also require dark 8 hours a day to set fruit.

Temperature: Summer crop. The ideal temperature is about 80° F [26 C], but they're fine down to 60° F [16C]. A sunny window helps.

Nutrients: Growing hydroponically, goes through five stages.

1. Very weak for germination and the first 2 weeks after that (about 3 weeks total).
2. Then gradually switch to vegetative growth stage nutrient mix.
3. Then transition mix for a week.
4. Then flowering and fruiting stage mix for the remainder of the plant's life.
5. When ripening fruit, mix the nutrients 10% stronger.

Stronger nutrients is the hydroponic equivalent of withholding water to improve flavor.

If you have an EC meter, try EC 0.6 for 3 weeks, EC 1.8 to 2.0 thereafter, up to 2.2 for ripening. Tomatoes are sensitive to the nutrients getting too acidic, and the plants themselves make the reservoir more acidic. Ideally, you'd keep the pH at 6.5, but it tends to drift down from there.

Dump and replace nutrient reservoir every week, and top up the reservoir with half-strength nutrients between refills. If the reservoir gets too low, the remaining nutrients in it are likely toxic, and the plant's lower leaves will brown and die. But tomatoes drink a lot. A reservoir less than a gallon may need topping up daily.

Starting: Germinates in about 7 days at room temperature – a warm spot speeds this up. Soak seeds in lukewarm water for a few hours before planting in soil.

Harvesting: Wait until the fruit is completely red, then wait another couple days for it to get even deeper crimson (or whatever color your variety is). Especially growing hydroponically, indoors, or under artificial lights, tomato flavor can be vapid if the fruit isn't allowed to ripen on the vine long enough. Don't despair if the first-picked tomatoes have disappointing flavor. This is almost always true of tomatoes, indoors or out. Later fruit taste better.

Pruning: Lots. The first pruning comes when the plant has five true branches above the seed leaves, plus a growing tip above the fifth branch. Just above that fifth branch, snip off the growing tip of the plant. This makes the plant branch out below. Beyond that, the arcane art of tomato pruning is debated – with diagrams, passion, and competing theories – across the Internet. Essentially, you need to prune the plant into a shape that will stay well-lit in your growing area. But the more you prune, the more you'll need to prune, and the more flower buds you'll cut off. Nobody likes to cut off flower buds – and their future tomatoes. And nobody likes to cut off healthy green branches. But if the branches are too dense, light and air can't circulate to the interior. It's a long-lived plant. You have plenty of time to explore your options. Cut off yellow leaves promptly.

Support: Tomato fruits are heavy, and a broken stem is one of those tomato heartbreak events. In a pot, some time before the first fruit set, drive a stake into the pot. Once there are small fruit forming, tie the vine to the stake just above a clump of fruit with a strip cut from pantyhose. The strategic art of supporting tomatoes is also diagrammed and debated throughout the Internet. In an Aerogarden, use the trellis system on the main stems, and also tie the vines to the lamp arm and trellis with strips of pantyhose. Using other hydroponic rigs, you'll have to figure out something. The vines need support before the fruit get heavy. Or they will break.

Pollinating: There are few self-pollinating tomatoes – you need to help out, or no fruit will set. When the flowers open, gently rub the nose of each flower with finger or soft-bristled paintbrush. Gently shaking the plant can also work to move the pollen, if there are too many flowers for individual attention, as with a cherry tomato.

Comments

Choosing a Tomato Variety

I'm not a fan of growing determinate tomatoes indoors. Unfortunately, most truly compact *"container"* tomato varieties are determinate.

In case you're new to tomato growing, tomato varieties come in three different fruiting strategies. An *indeterminate* tomato plant never stops growing. It ripens fruit along the way, for small but continual harvests. I like that. It takes 13 to 17 weeks to harvest my first tomato – once the plant starts delivering, I want months of regular tomato supply for my table.

In contrast, a *determinate* tomato sets a lot of fruit all at once, then ripens them all at once. It puts all of its energy into this crop, to the detriment of the vines. Then you harvest the fruit when they ripen, all within a few weeks. The tomato plant is mortally wounded by putting all of its energy into fruiting. It might or might not bear a weaker, second crop – after another month or so wait. This is a great harvest plan for making tomato sauce. For having a continual supply of salad tomatoes, not so much.

The third growth strategy is *"semi-determinate"*, which means somewhere between indeterminate and determinate. The semi-determinate tomatoes I've grown produce a trickle of tomatoes along the way, and never really stop, but also set a walloping big main crop. For indoor crop purposes, this is also not ideal.

Park's better bush tomato, a compact indeterminate, growing in deluxe crop pen.

The reason this matters is that almost all "container" sized tomatoes are determinate. In contrast, most indeterminate tomatoes get huge – like, up to 8 feet tall [2.5m] – not a feature we treasure for indoor growing. You can certainly prune them smaller, but not small enough.

Another basic distinction between tomato varieties is *"hybrid"* vs. *"heirloom"* or *"open-pollinated."* If you save the seeds from an heirloom tomato, you can grow the same tomato variety from the seeds. With the hybrids, not so. Though I love the movement towards growing heirlooms and saving seeds, I don't know of any heirloom tomato varieties that meet my indoor growing criteria. Tiny Tim is a popular determinate indoor heirloom tomato – good yields on a small plant – if you must have an heirloom. If you find a good compact indeterminate heirloom, please let me know.

But hybrids usually have disease resistance bred in, great vigor, bigger yields, and some good ones have been developed with the compact indeterminate body plan. In general, I recommend saving the heirloom tomato growing for outdoors, and growing a few hybrid tomato plants alongside them to ensure a crop. Essentially, without the bred-in disease resistance, heirlooms just die easier.

Do heirlooms taste better? Only if you can harvest some. The hybrid varieties recommended above taste great, as good as the best tomatoes I've ever bought or grown outdoors.

Seeds vs. Transplants vs. Clones

If you start a tomato project during the spring planting months in your area, you can buy tomato plants already a month or so old, ready to be transplanted out in the summer garden – or in your home. This can cut a month or more off your long wait for a harvest. I've seen some of my recommended varieties for sale at local plant nurseries or big box stores that carry a wide selection, though they aren't the most common tomatoes. In the Northeast, indoor growing temperatures aren't so different from summer conditions. Nursery plant selection will vary by region, by what tomatoes are suitable for local conditions. Hint: if your season regularly features 100° F weather, local nurseries may not carry any tomatoes suited for indoor growing. They'll carry heat-tolerant tomatoes instead. Likewise short-season regions may only carry early-bearing determinate tomato plants.

But if you can buy a plant, you can shave a few weeks off the wait for harvest. Or if you grow a suitable tomato variety outdoors, you can clone a tomato for indoor growing toward the end of the season.

With cloning, you can use a transplant even if your indoor project is hydroponic. Tomato plants are easy to clone. Cut off a growing tip section of the vine, about 9" [25 cm] long, with a razor or sharp scissors. This section of plant is called a "cutting." With a small transplant, this is simply the top of the seedling. Clip off the lower leaf-branches from the cutting. You're not just being tidy – the cut branches are the sites that have the ability to grow new roots.

Put the cutting in a jar of water, so that the water reaches at least 4 inches (8 cm) up the cutting, covering the cut branch spots. Place the jar somewhere it gets enough light to not-die, but not in direct sunlight. You don't need rooting hormone for this. Tomato vines love to grow new roots. Refill with fresh water every day or so, preferably the well-aerated water from your kitchen tap. Within

10 to 14 days, you'll see nice roots developing. You can transfer this rooted cutting directly into a hydroponic rig, with mild vegetative nutrients to start. Or, wait until the root system is a little more advanced and transplant into soggy potting mix in a pot. Keep a freshly potted clone out of direct sunlight or harsh lights for a few more days, to let the roots acclimate, then introduce to bright light gradually.

Ripening

Tomatoes ripen in response to ethylene gas. A ripening tomato produces this gas, so tomato-ripening often seems to spread as a contagion. Green bananas also produce a lot of ethylene. Try placing a green banana near a clump of big-enough tomatoes to kick-start the ripening. This can be especially helpful when growing determinate tomatoes.

Beginner Advice

Tomatoes are not a beginner's project. Please, gain experience first by growing something easier.

Peppers

Recommended Varieties: Most varieties work for indoor growing, about 28" tall or less. I like carmen peppers, a super-sweet hybrid horn shaped fruit, and mini red stuffing peppers, a 1 to 2 inch heirloom bell pepper, and lunchbox or yum-yum small sweet horn peppers. From other people's grows, the ultra-short Ace bell pepper also works well, and hot jalapeños, Big Jim and Anaheim green chilis.

Soil vs. Hydroponic: Whichever you prefer.

Time: About 17 weeks for ripe red peppers, 15 weeks for green, from seed. The timing isn't much affected by conditions.

Soil: 16 quarts of ordinary potting mix (no moisture control) in a 14" self-watering pot. Dwarf jalapeños might fit 2 to 3 plants in one pot. A few tablespoons of limestone or dolomite mixed into the soil helps, if you have it. Peppers prefer soil more basic (as opposed to acidic), and enjoy extra calcium.

Fertilizer: Can use tomato fertilizer.

Water: Keep the self-watering pot reservoir topped up, except when ripening fruit. When ripening, let the reservoir run dry between watering – pepper flavor thrives on adversity. This is especially important for hot peppers to develop their heat.

Light: Bright, 14 hours a day, but not as bright as tomatoes. Using purely artificial lights, try one 23 W 6500K CFL for a baby plant, and work up to four 23W CFLs arranged around a single plant as it grows, trying to get intensely bright light within 6" of the plant, on all sides. Or, six 23W CFLs for two pepper plants. From the time the plant begins forming its first buds, one third to one half of the light should be 4100K, the rest 6500K. LED lights would also work, of similar lumens. If using a sunny window, augment with artificial lights in winter. Six-tube fluorescent T8 lights are intense enough for most peppers. Four-tube T5 lights are certainly intense enough. Peppers also require dark at least 8 hours a day.

Temperature: Summer crop. The ideal temperature is about 80° F [26 C], but they're fine down to 60° F [16 C]. Again, a sunny window helps. If temperatures fall below 50° F [10 C], baby pepper fruit drop off the plant.

Nutrients: Growing hydroponically, goes through five stages, with somewhat stronger nutrients than for tomatoes.

1. Very weak for germination and the first 2 weeks after that (about 3 weeks total).
2. Then gradually switch to vegetative growth stage nutrient mix.

3. Transition mix for a week.

4. Flowering and fruiting stage mix for the remainder of the plant's life.

5. When ripening fruit, mix the nutrients 10% stronger.

Strengthening the nutrients is the hydroponic equivalent of withholding water to improve flavor.

If you have an EC meter, try EC 0.6 for 3 weeks, EC 1.8 vegetative, EC 2.0 thereafter, up to 2.2 for ripening. Mix nutes to a pH of 6.5, and try to keep them between pH 6.0 and 7.0. Note that you can grow peppers in EC up to 2.8. I haven't found much advantage to doing so, however.

Dump and replace nutrient reservoir every week, and top up the reservoir with half-strength nutrients between refills. If lower leaves get brown and crispy, probably the nutrients are too strong. Give the plants fresh water for a couple days, then refill with weaker nutrients.

Peppers don't require stronger nutrients than tomatoes. If growing both, they can share a weaker tomato-strength nutrient reservoir.

Starting: Germinates in about 10 days at room temperature – a warm spot will speed this up. Soak seeds in lukewarm water for a few hours before planting in soil.

Harvesting: A matter of taste. Peppers grow to their terminal size, then stay the same outer size but grow thicker walls, then ripen several weeks later. The color stages through all this depend on the variety. But a typical red bell or horn pepper goes through various shades of green, then ripens to red. Many people like their bell peppers green – when the walls thicken. I like my peppers at their sweetest. For that, I wait until the pepper is fully red, then wait a few more days for the red to deepen.

Pruning: Not necessary. Just grow a variety short enough for your growing space.

Support: Tie up the main stem for support, at least. Peppers like being crowded together, so long as each plant gets enough light. They can provide mutual support.

Pollinating: You need to help out, or no fruit will set. Fortunately, it's easy. When the flowers open, gently rub the nose of each flower with finger or soft-bristled paintbrush. Gently shaking the plant also works to move the pollen.

End Game: Peppers can live a long time – years. If your plant stops producing flowers, try giving it a rest for a couple weeks, then feed it some fertilizer and see if it might start producing again. The hydroponic equivalent would be a couple weeks of mild vegetative phase nutrients, then return to fruiting phase again.

Comments

Peppers are much easier to grow than tomatoes. They're beautiful plants, not particularly susceptible to disease, and most varieties are a convenient size and shape for growing indoors. You can speed the project up by buying a transplant pepper seedling in-season. Pepper plants can also be cloned, but it won't save any time.

I grow both hybrid and heirloom peppers. Heirloom pepper seeds are especially simple to save. Just grow a pepper to full ripe size, and dump the seeds onto a paper towel to dry for a few days. Then label a plastic baggie with the date, and store in a cool dark place, as with all seeds.

Pepper seeds are generally only good for 2 years, much shorter than most seeds, which stay viable for up to 5 years.

An unusual feature of peppers is that you can taste the effects of cross-pollination in the current generation. The cross-bred seeds seem to dictate the fruit development, instead of only the seed the plant was grown from. You can grow sweet peppers and hot peppers side-by-side. But where their branches intermingle and they cross-pollinate, you'll get some hot-sweet cross fruit.

Unlike many plants, peppers love being transplanted to bigger pots, even when they're loaded with fruit. This can be useful, as the different sized plants gradually need more light and room. I've had pepper plants go through up to 4 transplants. They like it. So my potted pepper plants start out in little 4 inch pots, and work their way up.

Project: Deluxe Crop Pen

This deluxe version of the crop pen can be used for tomatoes or peppers, or even cucumbers. It provides more growing room, light flexibility, and sturdiness than the simple crop pen and Aerogarden surround presented in Chapter 5, to allow you to grow bigger tomato plants. The base instructions are for a tomato plant, with peppers given as the variation.

Deluxe crop pen, lights and boards secured onto wooden utility shelving.

Need for the pot:

- Tomato seeds or transplant for a compact indeterminate tomato ($2 or more)
- 4" diameter starter pot, if growing from seed (16oz plastic with drainage holes)
- 14" diameter self-watering pot, capacity 16 to 20 quarts of soil (~$10)
- Potting mix, ordinary Miracle Gro or other fluffy container mix (~$8)
- Mulch (newspaper will do, if you don't have wood mulch)
- Organic tomato fertilizer – such as Tomatoes Alive! (~$7)

Need for the pen:

- IKEA IVAR, GORM, or HEJNE shelving unit, approx. 35"x 19.5" x 70" IKEA product offerings vary – but they sell wooden storage shelves
- Up to 8 hanging lamp cords ($40 IKEA, includes screw hooks)
- Heavy-duty timer (3-prong grounded outlet)
- 8-plus outlet surge protector strip
- Long twist-ties and screw-in hooks for cord management
- 8 CFL bulbs, 23W or so, 4 x 6500K, 4 x 4100K (~$40)
- Or whatever lights you prefer
- 3 foam core boards, 20" x 30" (50cm x 76cm) (~$10)
- Push-pins or tacks

The Plant

In-season, you can shave about a month off your wait for harvest by buying a transplant tomato – husky cherry or better bush mid-size are ideal. Out of season, you need to grow from seed, selecting a variety less than 3 feet tall (1m).

If you don't have a transplant-sized plant, first we'll grow one, then transplant it into the large pot. It's important to start the plant in two stages this way, to get a strong and short tomato vine.

√ **Tip:** If you smoke, wash hands before touching tomato plants.

It's a good idea to wash your hands before touching a tomato plant, because they're so susceptible to disease. This is crucial if you smoke, because tomato plants can catch tobacco mosaic virus from the tobacco in cigarettes.

To grow a tomato transplant, soak 3 seeds for a few hours in lukewarm water before planting to help them germinate faster. Half-fill a small starter pot with potting mix, and place in a bowl of lukewarm water to soak water up into the soil – add a little water to the top to speed this up. If you don't have a starter pot, you can use a very clean and opaque 16 oz plastic container [500 ml] such as a ricotta cheese or sour cream container, and drill drainage and watering holes in the bottom.

When seeds and soil are both well-soaked, plant the seeds 1/4" deep [0.5cm], spaced around the pot. Place the pot back into the empty bowl or some plastic container, to catch drainage and for bottom-watering later. Cover the pot with plastic wrap, place in a warm spot, and germinate in the dark. Keep the soil moist but not soggy until the seedlings emerge, in about 8 days.

When seedlings emerge, remove plastic wrap and move to bright light. When seedlings are 2" to 3" tall [5 to 7 cm] and have true leaves, not just seed leaves, pick the best plant and snip the rest off at the base with scissors. There's only room for one compact tomato plant in this crop pen.

When the seedling is tall enough that its branches clear the top of the starter pot, use scissors to clip off seed leaves that lie lower in the pot, then fill in around the stem with potting mix, and water that in. Tomatoes have the ability to grow roots along their stems, so this makes the seedling stronger, and shorter. At this point, also cut some newspaper or glossy junk mail, with a hole for the tomato stem. Place this over the potting mix as mulch. This prevents algae growth.

Tomato seedlings will be happy with one CFL, 6500K, until they're 3 weeks old from seed. By then they need two of the CFLs, both 6500K. Unless you have direct bright sunlight for at least 6 hours a day, do not grow a tomato transplant on a sunny windowsill. A lettuce seedling shelf is OK. Growing it in the crop pen is also fine. If tomato seedlings aren't kept in bright enough light, their stems "stretch", meaning they get tall and weak.

Transplant the seedling at age 4 weeks from seed, into your big self-watering pot. Or immediately, if you purchase a tomato transplant.

First prepare the pot. As with all self-watering pots, pack soil into the wicking section that reaches down into the reservoir, and water that in thoroughly. Add several more inches of soil, and water that layer in. Then fill the rest of the pot, and water in.

143

Planting a transplant, you want to bury the stem, to grow more roots and to keep the plant short. The two seed leaves and the lowest two leaf-branches are of no use to the adult plant (assuming the plant has at least 2 bigger leaf-branches at this point). So clip those off with scissors, but no more than you can actually bury in the depth of your pot. Don't clip off more than 1/3 of the foliage.

Dig a hole deep enough for the buried-stem transplant, and consult your tomato fertilizer package. Usually they direct you to mix 1 to 2 tablespoons of fertilizer into the transplant hole, and mix it into the soil. Do that.

Remove your transplant gently from its pot. Usually it is slightly "root-bound." That means the roots are coiling around the sides and bottom of the starter pot. Gently tease these roots loose a bit, to help them grow outwards. Otherwise new roots are blocked by a root barrier. Then put the plant into its hole. Fill the hole with potting mix, and water in. Do not cover green leaves with soil – either raise the plant, or clip the leaf branch.

Indeterminate plants only: We have one more bit of initial plant pruning. Sometime around week 4 to 5, your little plant should have more than 5 true leaf branches, with a growing tip above them along the main stem. Unless your plant is determinate, clip the growing tip off with scissors, just above the fifth true leaf branch. This encourages the plant to grow "suckers" - an extra branch at the base of each branch.

When you prune tomatoes, bear this in mind – each growth tip suppresses all lower growth tips on the same stem. Clipping off the growth tip, releases the lower suckers to grow into leafy, flowering branches (provided they have light). If you don't want more suckers, you have to pinch the suckers off too, about a week after clipping a growth tip.

As mentioned before, the arcane art of tomato pruning is a richly debated topic. The purpose of this initial stem-burying and pruning is to get as much strong fruiting plant as possible into a very short volume. After that, continue to prune as little as possible, but keep the plant healthy and well-lit, with air and light able to reach the plant's interior.

Determinate plants: With determinate tomatoes, the only pruning is the stem-burying. Then remove yellowed or burned leaves. Plus whatever pruning is necessary to make the plant fit the space available.

The Pen

These instructions use an IKEA GORM wooden shelving unit – I use this, and love it. IKEA comes out with a new brand of wooden storage shelves every few years, so you might need to rummage. At this writing, I see GORM, HEJNE, and IVAR variations.

What works well about the GORM is that you can position the shelves vertically to get a nearly 4 foot tall cavity in the middle [115 cm]. The strong wooden structure is easy to tack things to, and looks nice. I splurged an extra $17 for clip-on wire baskets, rubber end-caps to seal the feet against carpet steam cleaning, and a steel cross-brace for the back, for a grand total of $57 + sales tax for a substantial chunk of furniture. It would be a challenge to build an equivalent structure for less money in parts and lumber. Even if you need to pay shipping because you have no IKEA nearby, an IKEA unit might still be a cost-effective option.

I used stain and polyurethane on my GORM before I put it together. This was a bit of work, but my crop pen resides in my living room. So I made an effort to match my walnut-trim décor. You could also paint it with white semi-gloss, or simply seal the wood with polyurethane. The GORM is made of cheap unfinished wood, and looks it. I wouldn't leave it completely untreated. Spilled water, humidity, and hot lights are wood-warping conditions. The IVAR system looks less rustic, but it's also unfinished wood. HEJNE looks a lot like GORM.

Put the shelving unit together. Position two shelves at the bottom maybe 8 inches apart, and two shelves at the top. I spaced the top shelves to use wire storage baskets, but it doesn't greatly matter. If you bought the optional steel cross-brace, use it to strengthen the back of the big cavity in the middle. Place the shelving unit with its back to a wall, preferably white, or a window. If using against a window, please note that eye-searing light during the dark winter rush hour might elicit negative feedback from the neighbors.

The pen has two more components – light cords, and reflector sides. If you bought your hanging lamp cords from IKEA, each comes with some cord management clamps and screw hooks. We'll suspend the lights from hooks screwed into the wooden ceiling of the cavity – the second shelf from the top. Start by drilling a hole directly above the center, and screw a hook into it, to make sure you're drilling the right sized hole. I didn't have a power drill when I started this, and used an electric screwdriver with a spare screw instead. With effort, this could be done with a manual screwdriver.

145

Eventually, you want all 8 light sockets hanging from screw hooks. You can take care of that now while it's easy to get in there, without a big plant in the way. I suggest drilling 12 more holes in the shelf, evenly spaced and at least 4 inches from unit uprights, for a total of 13 hanging holes. The screw hooks can migrate between holes, to position lights where you want them. Also drill 4 holes spaced along one edge of the shelf, in the direction you want the power cords to go, and screw 4 hooks in there for cord guides.

For your first hanging lamp, insert a 6500K 23W CFL or an LED spotlight (or whatever you choose), and hang it from the center hook. Use a plastic clamp or twist-tie to secure a loop at the top of the cord, to set the light's vertical position 3" to 6" from the current top of your tomato plant [8 to 15 cm]. Take the power cord end and pass it through one of the hooks at the side of the shelf, then down to plug into the surge protector. The surge protector plugs into a timer, which plugs into a power outlet.

To keep the crop pen strong and stable, be sure to center the weight of any pots or reservoirs. For our potted tomato, this is simple. Put the big pot in the middle. Turn until the self-watering pot is easy to refill.

If you turn the light on, you'll notice immediately that one bare 23W CFL is already hard on the eyes. Yup, it's bright. Just imagine eight of them. That's what our final parts are for – side reflectors to keep that searing light on the tomatoes, not your retinas. Simply slide a 20"x30" foam core board into each side, cutting or tacking as necessary to get them to stay put and form sides for the cavity. You can center these 30" panels vertically, leaving ventilation above and below. You won't often need to adjust the sides.

In contrast, the front panel is removed every time you care for your plant. The long 30" dimension fits across the unit, giving you only 20" vertical coverage. So, you'll re-position this panel vertically as the plant grows and the lights shift upward. Place two push-pins into the wooden verticals where you want the current bottom of this panel to rest, probably around the height of your pot. Then rest the panel on the push-pins. Use a third push-pin touching (not through) one top corner, to keep the panel from falling off. Or, secure a top corner with a clamp. Unlike the bottom push-pins, whatever you use to secure the top needs to be removed and replaced frequently to reach the plant. So I use one push-pin instead of two, or a clamp if I have one free.

Growing On

Until the tomato has flower buds, use only the 6500K CFLs. Once it has tiny buds, use half and half, 6500K and 4100K. If using other lamps, the gist is to save red for later if you have a mix of bluer and redder lights. If all your lights have a red component, that's fine.

To keep the plant from stretching, you always want at least 1 or 2 of these lights directly above the plant. Distribute the rest around the sides of the plant, down to the midline, and some half-way between middle and top, trying to keep the hot surfaces 4 inches from the plant. You won't succeed – there isn't room enough for that, and the plant keeps growing. But try to prune branches back 2 to 3 inches from the light bulbs so that they don't burn and block the light from the rest of the plant. For a 2 to 3 foot tomato plant, you'll eventually want all 8 CFLs turned on, or whatever your equivalent is. For a smaller plant, you might only need 4.

Use the timer to give the tomato plant 14 hours of light a day. They also need 8 hours darkness per night. Lack of dark time can prevent tomatoes from setting fruit.

When flowers open, they need help with pollination. For a cherry tomato, it's enough to gently shake the plant. But for larger tomatoes, gently rub the nose of each flower with a fingertip or soft-bristled paintbrush. This works on cherry tomatoes, too.

Keep the plant watered. Reducing water during ripening can improve flavor. But if you reduce water too much, the fruit skins can crack.

Follow the directions on your fertilizer. Most suggest another feeding when the plant starts to flower. I find that the plants also need another feed after they've produced a harvest – probably once every two months. Too much fertilizer is risky, especially in soil. It isn't easy to remove fertilizer, and too much fertilizer makes the plant sick. So after the second feeding, only add fertilizer if the plant looks tired and yellowing, and don't do it too often.

Try to keep up with the pruning. You have limited space and light. The plant needs to be cut back to stay the right size, and allow light to penetrate to the inner stems.

Tomatoes take time. To grow from a pollinated flower – a fruit nubbin – to a ripe fruit can take 30 days for a cherry tomato, or 40 to 50 days for a medium sized tomato.

If the first fruit tastes vapid, don't lose heart. Consider the first fruit a practice attempt by the plant. Later fruit will taste better. Also, be sure to wait until the tomato is fully ripe before picking it. Assuming it's a red or pink tomato, it will first turn all-red, then deepen its color. So wait at least 3 days after the fruit is fully "red" before picking it – possibly longer.

If you need to pick fruit green (branch broke, necessary pruning, etc.), you can ripen them in a brown paper bag with a green banana, if they're big enough. Check every few days for signs of ripening. Remove the green banana when it turns yellow, and discard any tomatoes that show signs of rot.

Variations

Two clamp lamp hoods or spotlight bulbs would be helpful for the highest, middle lights, to direct light downward onto the tomato plant. For the remaining lower lights, I like bare helix bulbs, reflecting off the white sides of the enclosure. With LEDs, the equivalent might be spotlights above and flat panels on the sides. You get the idea – you're trying to surround the plant in a cage of painfully bright light.

Tomato

You can replace the self-watering pot with a hydroponic rig if desired. Some swear that hydroponic tomatoes are "better" than ones grown in soil. And if you keep the hydroponic nutrients perfectly tuned, there is certainly that opportunity.

But I find soil easier with tomatoes, because keeping hydroponic nutrients corrected takes continual effort, a couple times a week when the plant is big. It's far less work to add fertilizer every couple months, and otherwise just keep the plant watered. No hassles with water pH – just use plain tap water.

If you have a sunny window to donate to the project – and tolerant neighbors – you can cut your power bill by using all the sun available. You might be able to cut the number of lights in half that way – but probably no more than that, for full-size tomatoes. Outdoors, full-sized tomatoes need full direct sun 6 hours a day – 8 hours for beefsteak tomatoes. It's highly unlikely that a sunny window can provide that much light indoors without an artificial light assist, especially in winter. Cherry tomatoes can ripen with less light, but their flavor might suffer.

The crop pen also excels for growing indoor/outdoor tomatoes. More on that in the next chapter.

Pepper

The same crop pen works well for peppers. There are some differences.

First, with peppers, don't bury the stem. They don't have the ability to root along their stems. Most peppers are a convenient size for this crop pen, anyway, only 18" to 28" tall [45 to 70 cm].

It takes 6 weeks, not 4, to grow a pepper transplant from seed. They sprout very slowly in cool temperatures – up to 3 weeks. So germinate them in the warmest spot your house has to offer. Like tomatoes, they don't need light until they sprout.

This crop pen fits two pepper plants with ease, one in each of two self-watering planters. Two normal-sized pepper plants need only 6 CFLs combined. With a dwarf pepper plant (less than 18 inches or 45 cm tall), you might be able to fit 2 or 3 plants in each self-watering pot. You could try three in one pot, two in the other, then remove one if it gets too crowded. The five plants together would still need only 6 CFLs. If growing one normal-sized pepper plant, use 3 or 4 CFLs. As with tomatoes, when flower buds develop (when you can see white petals developing on the buds), add 4100K lights.

Peppers could also grow hydroponically in the crop pen. Peppers are a great deal more tolerant of nutrient strength, and don't ruin the the pH of their own water the way tomatoes do. So I don't have a strong preference for soil over hydroponics on peppers, the way I do for tomatoes. However, I have aphids, and aphids seem to adore hydroponically grown peppers. The aphids won – I grow peppers in soil.

Under indoor conditions, peppers may set a big crop, then seem to stop, exhausted, after harvest. Give them some fertilizer and a couple weeks rest. They'll likely recover and add another tier of leaves, with more buds, and set another harvest. Peppers aren't really *determinate* like some tomatoes are. But they don't go back and create new flower buds at old leaf junctures.

Peppers often "drop" their first fruits, set from their first flowers. Do what you can to make the plant happy, but don't worry too much about it. Eventually some of the fruit will "stick" and develop.

Only prune peppers for some external reason, like not enough space. Like tomatoes, pruning off a growth tip releases lower sapper branches to grow. Unlike tomatoes, this fact isn't very useful in practice.

Pepper fruit grow to their final external size, and can then sit there without ripening for a month or more. They are changing during this time – the walls thicken, the seeds develop, their color may go through phases, the fruit develop sugars, etc. Getting light onto the fruit can help this process along, but it takes time. If you like peppers green, and pick one too early, you may find it has thin walls and tastes terrible. Just give this green-ripening phase enough time. Or whatever color your particular variety of pepper gets, just before ripe. Some pepper varieties go through several radical color changes along the way. For instance, the popular banana pepper starts out green, turns banana yellow for the "green-ripening" equivalent phase, then turns scarlet, and eventually crimson when fully ripe. Other peppers add white, cream, orange, yellow, purple, or brown stages to their color repertoire.

If you grow a very small dwarf tomato plant, you could fit a tomato pot and a pepper pot in the same crop pen. Just set them out at the same transplant stage. From seed, that means planting the pepper 2 weeks earlier than the tomato. After transplant, they'll have about the same light needs at about the same time, with more light on the tomato. Fairy Tale eggplant would also make a compatible pen-mate for peppers. Both plants take 6 weeks to reach transplant size from seed, with similar light needs.

Peppers and eggplant are also excellent candidates for indoor/outdoor growing, coming up next.

Summing Up

Great-tasting tomatoes and peppers are the holy grail of many gardeners. Growing them indoors is possible, but not easy. They take months to reach harvest, and a lot of light. Other than that, peppers can be relatively plug-and-play. But for great tomatoes, that's just the beginning. Tomatoes take continual maintenance, especially to keep them bonsai'd into the available lighting.

This chapter describes recommended varieties and techniques for both crops, and finishes up with a deluxe crop pen project, equal to the task of growing these most demanding of summer favorites indoors.

Gee, that takes a lot of light. Wouldn't it be nice if you could grow the plants to almost ripening indoors, then kick them outside into the summer sun to ripen?

I do it every year. Next chapter: indoor-outdoor growing.

Indoor Salad

Chapter 9
Indoor / Outdoor Growing

Do you have some growing space outdoors? Like, any at all? Even room for a single 14" pot by the door or in the driveway? Space for a windowbox or two? A little scrap of flower garden?

If so, indoor growing can help you get maximum yield out of very little space, or very little growing season. The idea is simple. Young plants take up less room, and need less light, than mature plants. This is as true of lettuce as tomatoes. Most crops can be grown inside and transplanted outdoors when there's an available spot and weather conditions suitable for them to thrive.

Of course, you can buy transplants – in season. But what is "in season"? Plant nurseries and big box stores carry what most people plant, at the time most people plant them – transplants for spring. If you're trying to get maximum salad production out of a few windowboxes, it would be nice to have ongoing replacements, right into fall. And if you want a long season of tomatoes or peppers, ideally you transplant out a plant that already has fruit set and needs the intense summer sun to ripen them. A tomato or pepper of that maturity is already 2 to 3 months old. You can buy them. The selection is usually limited, and they often come with a price tag of $20 or more apiece.

There are also outdoor growing problems you can assist with an indoor-outdoor approach. For instance, here in shoreline Connecticut, spring is brief and cool, with unpredictable frost dates and freak heat wave days. Then regardless of how late our winter lingers, full summer arrives right on time.

This is a grab-bag chapter of tips for getting the most vegetable production out of limited outdoor space.

Hardening Transplants

A word to the wise on all indoor-to-outdoor transplants. Be sure to harden transplants gradually, before planting them outdoors. Sunshine is much stronger than indoor lights. Gently reared stems can't withstand spring kite-flying weather and thunderstorms. Especially early spring transplants, like pansies and spinach, are going out to a much harsher environment than the cozy womb of a seedling shelf at human room temperature. A few days – or a week, depending on local spring winds – ramping up from a sheltered location to withstanding full outdoor conditions, gives young plants time to toughen up those leaves and stems to withstand life in the real world.

To harden plants, move them to a sheltered location outdoors for only a couple hours the first day. Gradually work up to the conditions the plant will face when transplanted outdoors full-time, over the course of a few days to a week, depending on how fragile the plant is.

Tomatoes and Peppers

These plants take a long time, in very bright light, to produce fruit. But they take half as much light to reach fruiting size – and even to develop the fruits to half-size. If you plant out normal 4 to 6 week old transplants in spring, you generally have another 60 to 85 day wait for harvest. Around here, that delivers the earliest ripe full-size tomatoes in late July, and peppers in August. I do grow transplants of that size – and I grow dozens of my own vegetable transplants, plus dozens of flower transplants, all in a modest little two-T8 fluorescent light seedling shelf. But I also grow a couple more advanced indoor-outdoor plants each year, usually peppers, but sometimes also tomato or eggplant.

I harvest my first outdoor sun-ripened peppers from those plants in May or June. They provide a trickle of harvest to cook with until my main-season peppers are ready 2 to 3 months later. And that's from the plants I grew specifically for indoor-outdoor growing. Any peppers I have indoors gets boot outside in spring. I've planted them in September and harvested several rounds before they migrated outdoors as mature plants.

This is simple, because these three vegetables love to be transplanted into better conditions. That's not true of all plants – but it is for peppers, tomatoes, and eggplant. No matter how mature, they'd love to get more light. If you can also offer them more root space, so much the better.

The only trick is that you need to harden the plants gradually to outdoor conditions – and make sure those outdoor conditions are suitable for them before they move out full-time. For instance, peppers cannot stand temperatures below 50° F [10 C]. They won't die, but they will drop all their fruit, which defeats the purpose. For the earliest possible outdoor-ripened fruit, this means the plant might have to move in and out until the night-time temperatures gradually stabilize above 50° F. Tomatoes and eggplant don't drop their fruit so readily, but they don't grow much below 50° F, either – they just endure. Below 40° F [5 C], even surviving gets chancy.

For an example, say I wanted to get maximum mileage out of a crop pen like the one in the previous chapter, to produce early outdoor fruit. I could start two normal-sized pepper plants in January, and a tomato at the end of February, in my seedling shelf – which is already in full swing by January growing slow pansy transplants. The peppers would move to the crop pen by mid February, and stay until nearly April. By then, my frigid west-facing window is not so frigid, and the wan winter south-western light, changes to bright enough western spring sun to sustain a pepper. The peppers move to window, and the tomato takes over the crop pen for a couple months. By mid-May, all of these plants can move outdoors full-time, with fair-sized fruit already developing – giving harvests in May and June. With luck, those early harvest plants can continue bearing outdoors through early October.

Does indoor-outdoor imply outdoor-indoor? Not really. Going outdoors is usually a one-way trip for plants. If you bring a big plant indoors in the fall, in an attempt to extend the season, you'll also bring an awful lot of bugs inside. Insect pests are hard to control indoors, without their natural predators. Tomato plants are often also diseased by the end of the season. And there is no real way to "soften" plants for weaker indoor lighting, to reverse "hardening" for full sunlight.

That said, I gave my mother a carmen pepper plant. She recently brought it back indoors for its second winter, after its second productive summer on her deck. I don't expect that to work with every plant. But it does for some.

Peas and Potatoes

What do these two crops have in common? Not much, except that they're both spring crops. And as mentioned, spring is in short supply around here. So to grow these crops at all locally, they need a little help to lengthen our dubious spring season. They don't transplant well. But you can still get them started growing indoors, then plant them.

Peas take weeks to germinate in cold soil – possibly over a month. And they're supposed to be planted about 6 weeks before the average last spring frost. Of course the soil is cold. They also die rather promptly once the weather turns hot. It took a couple years of failed pea harvests for me to catch on to this one. Simply pre-germinate the pea seeds in a cup of water. First stage, let them soak for only 3 hours, in lukewarm water. Then drain off the water, but leave the pea seeds wet.

Several times a day, rinse the peas again, leaving them wet but not sitting in water. Within a few days, the pea seed tap-root unravels from the pea seed – it is pre-germinated. When most of the peas have noticeable tap roots, plant them in their final outdoor location, with pea and bean inoculant, at whatever depth the package suggests.

Congratulations, your outdoor pea harvests can now begin 3 weeks earlier than they otherwise would have.

Peas come in at least four different types, by the way – snow peas, sugar snap peas, edible podded peas, and shell peas. I like them all. Sugar snap peas and edible podded give you the most edible food per plant. Fresh-picked peas are a sweet delight that you cannot buy – not from supermarkets, and not from farm markets either. The sugars in peas turn to starches within hours. Good chefs use frozen peas, not fresh, because of this. Peas take a lot of room, and they're not very productive. But I love them fresh and grow them whenever I can. Highly recommended.

Potato plants naturally emerge from potato eyes. They do this in your cupboard whether you want them to or not. Most instructions for planting potatoes don't involve pre-sprouting them. But again, pre-sprouting them indoors can cut weeks off the time to harvest. Of course, you can plant good-tasting potatoes that have already voluntarily grown in the cupboard. But when doing this intentionally, pick some great-tasting and small potatoes, dampen them, and put them in a bowl in indirect sunlight. Dampen them again from time to time. If you have better luck sprouting potatoes in your kitchen cupboard, by all means, use that. You don't want whole potato vines to grow from them, but eyes grown out an inch [2 cm] is a great start. Then plant the whole potato as early as possible outdoors.

Oddly enough, potatoes are a practical crop to grow in limited space, using a potato-growing bag. These are cloth bags specially designed for the purpose. The bag's footprint can be as small as 18 inches in diameter [45 cm], though of course the full-grown plants are much bigger. This is a practical size to grow anywhere a potted tomato could grow.

Potatoes take an awful lot of potting mix. To cut costs, I cut the potting mix with perlite and free leaf compost from the town recycling center. You start the bag with 8 inch deep soil [20cm], placing 4 to 5 sprouted potatoes at 4 inch deep [10cm]. As the potatoes grow, you fill in around the stems with more potting mix, enriched with potato fertilizer, until the bag is full. Like their tomato cousins, potato plants can grow roots along the buried stems. In this case, they grow potatoes along with those roots. After the potato plants die off, plus a week or so, you empty the bags and retrieve the crop.

There are lots of potato varieties. My favorites are the waxy salad potato types, white, yellow, or red. My favorite red potato – Red Norland – can sometimes be found at the supermarket. The most common red potato is pink-skinned, but Red Norland is a deeper red. Another I've found only as seed potatoes, not in stores – Yellow Finn. This is another thin-skinned salad potato, yellow, rather flattened ovals, with a knob on one end. Absolutely delicious, not mealy at all, with a buttery flavor.

Melons and the Cucurbit Family

Cucumbers, melons, and squashes don't transplant nearly as well as tomatoes and peppers. Worse, what *"transplant"* means to them is a bit extreme. If you grow a cucumber in a self-watering pot, and then move the pot, the cucumber will experience a setback, production-wise. The cucurbit family has big leaves on sturdy, bent leaf-stems (petioles). They put energy into arranging their leaves just so, for optimal sunlight use.

Cucumbers take off when the weather suits their fancy, and not one day sooner. They don't have a programmed number of days of development the way tomatoes do. So there may be little to gain by starting them indoors or buying transplants. Just plant the seed where it is to grow, when the weather is warm enough for them. I only start cucumbers indoors when spring is especially late and cold.

The one exception in this family is melons – they are worth starting indoors or as transplants. Most cucurbits need to be transplanted a mere 2 weeks after planting the seed. Melons grow a bit slower, and can be started up to 4 weeks before hardening and transplanting to their final growing destination. If you need room to finish a spring crop first, or simply have a very short season for melons, 4 weeks can make a difference. In my case, the melon growing season is cramped indeed. Melons like it hot, and suffer if they get too wet when they're ripening fruit. There are small melons I can grow. But between insects, diseases, temperature, and rainstorms, my melon vines tend to fail in August, so I'm left with a very brief hot season. Which is wonderful for me, but not the melons.

Some small melon varieties I've successfully grown in containers are Gurney's Li'l Sweet Cantaloupe, Burpee's Sweet 'n Early Cantaloupe, and Park's Gold Bar melons. They seem to do best on my blacktop driveway, where it's hotter and their leaves stay dry. I give them a round tomato cage to climb on, and rest fruit on the potting mix or tied to the cage in panty-hose slings. Cantaloupe slip off the stem when ripe, and they are heavy. So I tie up big fruit in slings to prevent them from cracking as they fall to the pavement, or rolling away down the road.

Lettuce and Greens

This is a simple matter of geometry. Lettuce and other greens are very small plants for the first month of their lives. If outdoor space is at a premium, you can grow transplants for the first month of their lives indoors, and plant them out to finish growing to their full size. A couple 6-packs take up less room than a dinner plate, and most windowsills provide enough light for these seedlings. Then you can transfer them outside to a windowbox or other habitat as space becomes available.

Reserve a slot or three for some basil, dill, or parsley. They grow nearly as fast as lettuce, and can be tucked into a scrap of flower garden. Herbs and peppers are pretty in flower gardens. Tomatoes not so much. Try to hide them in the back. Tomatoes and potatoes look so lovely when they're young. They're an eyesore by ripening time, though.

Transplants in General

If you have a special angle – such as rare plant seeds, tricky plants to grow, grafted tomatoes, school fund-raising, a local unmet need, transplants out of season, or whatever – growing transplants might be a fun little money-making venture. As an indoor home grower, you can't compete with real plant nurseries and their automation for pansy demand in spring. But if the big nurseries aren't going after indoor tomato demand in October, or even outdoor lettuce demand in September, there's no reason you couldn't, provided you have a way to bring the product to market.

Summing Up

Indoor growing tricks can help you get maximum mileage out of even a little outdoor growing space. Many crops can be successfully started as transplants under artificial lights or on a bright windowsill. Be sure to harden them gradually to outdoor conditions before transplanting.

With tomatoes and peppers the usual "transplant" age is 60-plus days before first harvest. But these slowpoke favorites can be grown bigger indoors in containers, and then transferred outdoors to ripen and produce fruit all summer. Most crops can't transplant outdoors at that extreme. But even peas and potatoes can pre-germinate indoors, to get a head start on the outdoor season. You can grow your own normal-sized transplants indoors for lettuce, other greens, herbs, and melons, as well.

Whatever growing projects you pursue, I wish you the best of luck! And I hope to see pictures of your grows online. You're not alone. And this book isn't over. There is more content all the time at my site aerogardenmastery.com. And there are growers all over the world, just like you. We're happy to answer questions on all the many gardening forums. I hope to see you there.

Links to websites and products mentioned can be found on my website at
gingerbooth.com/indoorsaladlinks

Best wishes,

Ginger Booth

I hope you enjoyed *Indoor Salad*,
and got new ideas to empower your gardening.

Planted anything yet?

Please

If you enjoyed *Indoor Salad*, I'd deeply appreciate a
review on Amazon. Thank you.

Books by Ginger Booth

Nonfiction

Indoor Salad: How to Grow Vegetables Indoors
E-Cigarettes 102: DIY E-Liquid

Fiction

The Calm Act series
End Game
Project Reunion
Martial Lawless
Tsunami Wake

Feral America series

Feral Recruit
Feral Agent
Feral Courier
Feral Carolina

Calm Act Genesis prequels (ebook only)
Civilly Disobedient **
Dust of Kansas **
Ebola Day
Road to Humble Texas

** To receive two prequel ebooks **free**, join my reader group at
gingerbooth.com/freebooks

161

Printed in Great Britain
by Amazon

42643129R00099